Dog Sports Skills,

Play:

First published in 2015 by:

Fenzi Dog Sports Academy Publishing

Copyright © 2015 Denise Fenzi & Deborah Jones, Ph. D.

All uncredited photos © 2015 Denise Fenzi & Deborah Jones, Ph. D.

Designed by: Rebeccah Aube | www.pawsink.com
Paws & Ink! A Creative Blend of Dog Training & Graphic Design

ISBN NUMBER: 978-0-9887818-4-9

Dog Sports Skills, Book 3: Play!

by Denise Fenzi & Deborah Jones, Ph.D.
Copyright 2015

TABLE OF CONTENTS

Acknowledgements

From Deb and Denise:

We have found the +R dog training community to be filled with kind, funny, intelligent and talented individuals who support us in ways too numerous to mention. Thanks to each of you for all that you give to us both as trainers and as individuals. We value you very much.

We would like to thank our editor, Crystal Barrera, and our creative book designer, Rebeccah Aube, for their patient and thoroughly competent approach to each of our books. We couldn't have done it without you!

To all of our friends in the dog world who have contributed fantastic photos to make this book possible, thanks! You have made our book much much richer with your generosity.

From Denise:

This book is dedicated to Cisu, the master of play! Your special talent was figuring out what I wanted and then patiently bringing me around when I was ready to learn. Thank you for that. Wherever you are, I hope you've found some wonderful new friends who recognize just how special you are. The whole +R community owes you.

And always, thank you to my husband, Millo, and my kids, Nick and Chris. Your never ending efforts to "balance" my life and get me away from my work are much appreciated!

From Deb:

I would like to dedicate this book to Copper, my soft, sensitive little Papillon. My heart dog. You taught me how to approach each dog and customize playful interactions accordingly. You also taught me that "less is more" when it comes to bringing out the playful side of a certain type of dog.

I'd also like to thank my FDSA students for allowing me the opportunity to work with them and their dogs. I learn so much from every single team. You guys inspire me to continue developing new ideas.

And Chris, as always, everything I do is about you.

A whole book on the topic of play? Is this really necessary? Isn't play, well… natural?

Play within a species is, indeed, natural. But even within a species, good play is learned by interacting with others. When human children learn to play, they start out supervised by adults who help them learn the rules so that all participants have a good time. They learn to express likes and dislikes, and if they aren't having a good time, they often walk away and find another play partner. They learn to select partners who enjoy the same activities that they do, and to avoid individuals who are unpleasant to interact with.

How about with dogs? As an observer, it appears to be the same, except dogs rely on body language over words. Puppies learn from adult dogs and littermates how to play, and when they aren't having a good time they too walk away and find more suitable play partners. This often turns into strong preferences for certain play partners over time. They learn the boundaries for acceptable play behavior, and they learn how to avoid other dogs they simply don't enjoy spending time with.

So what happens when different species attempt to play with one another? It's often very awkward! To play well across species requires a lot more attention to subtle details of body language and the intention of the other player. It is rare for humans to play well with another species unless they are highly in tune with their play partner or very motivated to learn, and dogs often appear to have the same struggles learning to play well with us.

Of course, some play partners make it easy. When a dog takes a ball, drops it in your lap, and backs up with an expectant look, most of us can figure out what is wanted. But how about dogs who would love to play games with us, but haven't learned to express themselves so clearly? That is where this book comes in.

You've probably figured out by now that the topic of play is vitally important to us. We believe that play is especially helpful when training performance dogs because of the way it can generate energy, enthusiasm, and engagement. It can help with stress relief, which is often needed in high-pressure competition settings. Play also gives you another way to appreciate your canine friends. It will allow you to do the same things with your dog that people like to do together (play games, share food, and interact personally). Developing excellent play can take your relationship with your dog to another level - maybe one you had no idea was possible!

Do you absolutely have to play with your dog in order to be an effective trainer? No, of course not - but you are limiting yourself if you don't take advantage of the many forms of play that are available to you. The more play skills you are able to develop, the greater your chances of creating a training program that will be highly enjoyable for both of you.

This book builds on the previous two books in this series. In Book 1: Developing Engagement and Relationship, we talked about establishing trust and a sense of teamwork between you and your dog. In Book 2: Motivation, we fleshed out the concept of motivation in great depth, from what it is to why you need it to be a successful force-free trainer. This current book, then, will dive into the specifics of using play-based motivators to maximum advantage.

To be motivating, your play must be interesting to your dog, and this is something you will learn together. Not only do you need to develop your dog's interest in a variety of forms of play, your dog must also know that you want to play! This is often easier said than done - and therein lies the value of this book!

This book will take a serious and extremely detailed look at the realities of play from the dog's point of view so that you can find a space that meets everyone's needs. We discuss tug, fetch, food play, and personal play at great length in the upcoming chapters. We will discuss how each of these types of play is distinct from one another, why you might want to use one over another, and then give you the nuts and bolts of how to develop the skills needed for each type. We will also offer some troubleshooting for common problems with each type of play.

And most importantly, we will encourage you to play with your dog! Not only will you add to your bank of motivators for training, you will have a good time. Both dog and trainer can finish a training session feeling energized and excited about what humans have known for thousands of years: people and dogs were made to be together!

About Us

Denise Fenzi

I am a professional dog trainer who specializes in building relationships in dog handler teams who compete in dog sports. My personal passions are Competitive Obedience and spreading high quality information about no-force (motivational) dog training. I travel the world teaching seminars on topics related to Dog Obedience and Building Drives & Motivation. Most of my time and energy is now focused on the development and growth of my online school for competition dog sports -- the Fenzi Dog Sports Academy. Check us out at www. fenzidogsportsacademy.com and see what we might have to offer you!

Deborah Jones, Ph.D.

I am a social and behavioral psychologist, full-time college professor, and dog trainer. My focus is on combining a thorough knowledge of the scientific aspects of learning with the art of applying that information to the effective training of dogs for dog sports. The effective and efficient application of learning theories and principles is still a work in progress for most dog trainers. I have enjoyed competing in Rally, Agility, and Obedience with my dogs over the years. Writing is one of my passions, along with the more recent addition of teaching online classes at Fenzi Dog Sports Academy.

Foreward
Play Stories

Teri Martin

My young vizsla Stella and I had a great first year together, but cracks began to show as we moved into more advanced competition. One weekend, I ended up in tears because my dog made it very clear to me that she wasn't interested in competing with me.

People told me I needed to get more serious with training. That Stella needed to know that she had a job to do and that work was not a choice. I wasn't so sure. Stella is a soft, easily frustrated dog, and my gut told me that she needed things to be fun if there were to be any chance of success.

We enrolled in an online heeling games class with Denise, and my big A-HA! moment came from these words:

"Play. A tiny bit of work. Play. Work. Etc. If she can stay engaged and playful in public, then she can work. And you will find that it is just as hard to get five minutes of continuous play as it is to get five minutes of continuous work. That's because they are both forms of engagement, and engagement (which excludes the environment) is a big deal."

I took those words to heart. A year later, we entered that same trial and rocked it with high in trial numbers, and even better, a wonderful feeling of being a team! Play is truly the glue that holds us together.

Lori Hansen

In the movie "The Princess Bride" the evil villain, Vizzini, keeps responding to frustration by exclaiming loudly, "INCONCEIVABLE!" To which the unflappable Inigo Montoya replies, "You keep using that word. I do not think it means what you think it means."

I should have named my dog Inigo, because I'm sure that's what he thinks every time I squeakily proclaim, "Wanna PLAY?"

As a serious rule-following control "enthusiast", play does not come naturally to me. Transitioning from correction-based to reinforcement-based training was easy; I'd rather have a teammate than an inmate any day. But taking the next step to playmate was another story. I thought play meant always being an over-the-top, exuberant, high pitched, baby talking freak show - and I was the kid who always took a book out to recess!

Play can be like that, but I've learned that there is more to play than that! I'm learning that play is not what you do. It's a state in which you, your dog, and pure joy converge in a mutually enjoyable moment. Will the connection be made with food, toys, tug, chase, petting, praise or even just the work itself? Fortunately, I've learned that I don't have to be the master of all fun. What I do need to be is a keen observer. I need to read what my dog is telling me, what he finds fun, and then respond appropriately. The result is a dog having as much fun doing obedience as he ever did doing agility!

So, if I may channel my inner Vizzini for a moment, let me just say this: Dog sports without play? INCONCEIVABLE!

Jacqueline Wilhelmy

Mer always loved toys. That was true. What she didn't seem to have was an interest in engaging with me with toys. She could amuse herself endlessly with toys, no human required. Once, when she was about 8 months old, I walked out of the dog park (because she didn't come when I called her), and waited outside. When I looked back in 30 minutes later, she was happily chasing tennis balls around all by herself. I sat down and cried.

Mer was incredibly independent from the day I brought

her home, and I didn't have the faintest idea how to train a dog. Mer was a handful. She also mouthed - a lot. I was told by some well-meaning folks that I had to show her who was boss, so I started rolling her over and holding her down. In response, she started snapping at me: when I reached for her, when I tried to punish her, when I bumped into her while she was sleeping. She wouldn't stay near me unless she was on a leash, and she didn't have any interest in food. She would even refuse to take steak from me!

I can't really say our relationship was bad, because we didn't have a relationship at all.

When Mer was a year-and-a-half old, we spent the summer working on a sheep farm. I guess the universe was watching out for us, because the person who owned the farm had an interest in dog training. She told me that I needed to knock off all the nonsense that made Mer see me as scary. She also told me that although not every dog will work for food or play fetch, I COULD use Mer's interest in toys to increase her responsiveness to my verbal cues.

I began to toss one toy after another for Mer. All she had to do was a single simple behavior like offering eye contact. I would stand out in the fields with a handful of Frisbees. I'd toss one, show her the next to entice her back, ask her to drop the first one, and then immediately throw the second Frisbee. I found that if I tossed a toy behind me and took off running, she would retrieve it and race ahead of me, then drop to the ground and wait for me to come get the toy.

She never did get the concept of fetching while I stood still, but she did develop a funny game of hitting a tennis ball back to me using the toy that she was holding in her mouth.

Our relationship didn't repair itself overnight, but slowly we made progress.

In the past two years, Mer has stood on the podium at multiple USDAA Regionals. She ran in PSJ Finals at her first Cynosports on her 6th birthday. And this past year was truly her year: she made finals in all of the events at Cynosports, placed 2nd in PGP and Biathalon, and placed 1st in Masters Series and Biathalon at the US Open!

One of my favorite photos of Mer is from the finals last year. In it, I am looking at the person who was manning the gate. And Mer is staring up at me, completely focused and still. I hadn't asked her to watch me, but she was looking to me for guidance anyways. Pretty amazing for the dog who would run the other way when I called her not that long ago!

And it never would have been possible, if not for one very special summer, when we learned to play.

Sue Yanoff

"Charm! What is wrong with you?!" I thought as I walked out of the Utility A ring with my 9th NQ in a row. I was almost in tears. Charm's performance got worse every time we trialed, and it was clear that she did not want to work any more.

It wasn't a lack of training, either. We trained a lot, and the worse she did, the more I corrected her. Unfortunately, the more I corrected her, the worse she got. This sucked all the joy out of training. Her attitude plummeted and we were circling the proverbial drain.

A few days after that trial, I found out about a four day obedience camp being offered by a trainer known for her positive training. I signed up. Those four days changed my dog training life. After a four-week break during which I thought a lot about what I had learned, I did two things: I re-trained all the utility exercises using positive reinforcement, and I made training FUN. Instead of just handing over food treats for good performance, I used the food for play. I teased Charm with the food, I threw the food, I made the use of food into a game. I also taught Charm how to play tug. We played before training, we played during training, and we played even when we weren't training.

One year later, I started showing Charm in utility again. She got her title in four shows.

Now we have a whole book dedicated to playing with your dog, and how to use play in training. I have no doubt it will be as good as Denise's and Deb's previous two books. I can't wait to read it.

Chapter One
Play is in the Eye of the Beholder

Good play is not measured by the techniques you use; all forms of play can be useful and helpful. Rather, good play is measured by the amount of enjoyment it generates between you and your dog. If a specific technique generates energy, engagement, and enthusiasm, then it is the right technique for your team.

This is great news because it means your dog doesn't need to be born loving a tug toy or tennis ball. In fact, the more you exercise your dog's interest in something, the more your dog is likely to develop a desire for that motivator. The more you play ball, the more your dog will want to play ball because it exercises his prey drive. The more you use food play, the more your dog will value it. The more you play tug, the more excited your dog will become at the sight of a tug toy. It is not unusual for dogs to grow in their love of a motivator simply through repeated positive exposures.

This book will suggest a wide range of options to try, with many different ways to use toys, food, physical interaction, and movement, but ultimately, your dog's opinion matters more than ours! Each team - a dog and a trainer - is unique. What makes sense for one team may well be a disaster for another. That's why we want to start by considering some of the factors that make you and your dog special, and how that might affect your choices when you play.

Your Dog's Natural Play Style

Dogs tend to be strong (or weak) in different aspects of the prey sequence - eye, stalk, chase, catch, kill, and consume. While there are exceptions, most dogs prefer to spend time in whatever part of the sequence that is most naturally enjoyable to them. This is important to understand because the games that dogs (and people) play are make-believe versions of the real thing. Your dog knows that when you play tug with a toy it's not a real rabbit - but it satisfies an innate need to engage in this type of activity. Likewise, your dog knows that when he is wrestling with you his goal is not to take you down and kill/consume you - but he likes to pretend, just like humans enjoy make-believe games.

Five week old Border Collie Helo already shows his strength in the stalking portion of the prey sequence.

This doesn't mean play is not valuable - it is - but learning to play at the right level of arousal is of great importance and also quite difficult to do. It takes time, mechanical skills, and studying your partner to get it right. And since each dog is an individual, the process does not end after you learn with one dog. You have to start over with each new partner!

For this reason, it can be really helpful to consider your dog's natural play tendencies

These Ibizans love to play chase with each other. They love to chase humans, too!

before you involve yourself in the game. Does your dog like to chase when playing with other dogs? Then look for games that relate to chase - chase the ball, chase the toy on a long line, chase the food, chase the human. Does your dog like to wrestle, tug and "fight"? Then look for games that relate to this tendency - fight to possess the tug, fight to get to the food, wrestle with the human. Maybe pretend to grab him and let him jump away!

Indigo plays with her canine friend - and with her mom!

Sin loves to play tug with both dogs and people!

More is Not Better

When Denise teaches seminars, she sees the following scenario rather frequently:

A quiet dog comes out on the floor to practice play skills with the handler. The dog is often doing anything but engaging with the handler. He may be staring off into the distance or sniffing the floor. The handler, anxious to develop good play skills, starts whooping, grabbing toys and hitting the dog's butt with them, calling him, poking at him, and basically doing everything but opening up the dog's mouth and shoving the toy in (though Denise has seen that too). After thirty very intense seconds, the handler abruptly stops and turns to Denise, and says, "See? He won't play!" Meanwhile, the dog appears relieved that the interaction is over.

This dog is showing avoidance and therefore is not ready to play with her handler just yet.

Repeat this phrase until you are convinced: MORE IS NOT BETTER. The goal is not to overwhelm your dog with your enthusiasm; that is no more effective than grabbing a shy child out from behind her mother's back and insisting that she play. Yelling "we're having fun! Aren't we having fun?!" does not make it true, because no, the child is not having fun. You're terrorizing her, and no good mother will allow you to do that to her child.

But with our dogs, we go all out with our noise and energy, ignoring the myriad ways they are trying to show us that they hate what we are doing. They sniff, turn away, cower, and actively avoid us when they see a toy emerging because they've begun to associate toys with being harassed. Worse yet, not only do toys become poisoned by association, but so does training time, working environments, and the trainer herself! A few months of this type of play training and you will be a good deal worse off than you were when you started. Even if your dog does "play," it's possible he has simply learned to engage with a toy as a way to escape the harassment. That doesn't mean he is enjoying the activity.

Taking the Fun Test

If you're not sure if your dog is playing for fun or because you insist, try this test:

Using a toy you think your dog loves, play in a way you think your dog enjoys. Then, stop and face your dog. Hide the toy behind your back, be silent, and don't move. Wait for three seconds. If your dog truly loved the activity, he will stare at you with an excited and open expression, or he might try to get the toy in an effort to re-engage in the activity. However, if he turns away or starts to sniff, then he is NOT looking for a way to cause you to re-engage; he is trying to leave you.

Curly remains focused when the toy goes away. He has passed the fun test!

Now repeat this activity with some food. Toss out a few cookies in random directions - run with the cookies, play with the cookies, hide a cookie between your legs for your dog to find, or encourage your dog to jump for those cookies! Now stop and simply face your dog for three seconds. What do you see? If your dog is focused on you with a bright and expectant face, then that's super; your dog is truly engaged and wants more! If your dog is ready to leave as soon as you stop actively engaging him, then maybe he's not really interested in your games.

And one last time, let's repeat this exercise with personal play. Go ahead, engage your dog using only your movements, personality, and enthusiastic interaction at whatever level of intensity you believe is most attractive to your dog. Again, after a period of time, stop and watch your dog carefully. Is your dog looking at you with bright eyes in the hopes that you'll re-engage, or wandering off to find something else to do after less than three seconds?

Curly is now taking the fun test for personal play; he passes!

In each scenario, you have a chance to learn about your dog. If he maintains contact for three seconds, then you can explode back into play - whatever you were doing was working for you! If your dog has left and you're trying to figure out how you'll re-engage, take a moment to re-evaluate your actions. Do you need to change how you are playing? Is the location appropriate for your dog's stage of play development? Did you simply play for too long and your dog needs a break?

Take the answers to heart.

In addition to using this simple test as a barometer of engagement, you can also use it to quickly assess which form of motivation is most potent to your dog under various circumstances. Which form of play does your dog prefer in your house? How about in your training room? The training hall across town? Since motivators can be hugely influenced by the alternatives and environmental factors (as discussed at length in our second book), this is a quick way to get some information about which motivators might make the most sense under any given set of circumstances.

If Kate continues to engage even after a break of a few seconds, then we know that personal play is a valuable motivator for her.

You cannot force a dog to enjoy interacting with you, but you can set up interactions that are positive and fun for your dog. You can do this by reading your dog's energy level and adding one notch up if you want more from your dog, or matching your dog's energy and taking it down one notch if you want less energy at that moment (we'll discuss this more in an upcoming chapter). You can quit while you're ahead - usually after less than a minute or two of interaction. You can learn to read your dog and respect his requests to stop if you're asking too much. In this manner you accomplish two goals: you can bring as much positive value to your motivators as is possible, and at the same time, you can build up your personal relationship with your dog.

Your Preferences Matter Too

If you think about it, you'll see that the games dogs play are the same ones that we humans play. This makes sense since we are both predators; we play chase, tug of war, hide and seek, wrestle, engage in mental contest games, and so on. And we have the same problems; sometimes we get over-aroused and flip into anger or aggression. This means that if play is supposed to be fun for the dog, it also needs to be fun for you. Training is not all about the dog; it's about the team. Both halves of the team must have their needs met in order for training to be the highly enjoyable and mutually satisfying event that it can be.

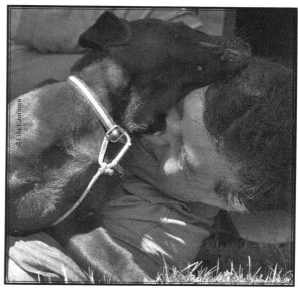
Who's having more fun, the puppy or dad?

If your dog is hurting you in play (and it is not a simple accident that can be ignored), then your play needs to change. If your 100-pound dog is jumping on you and knocking you to the floor, then your play needs to change. If your dog's preferred style of play is to run and chase and you have asthma, then your play needs to change. It doesn't matter what your fellow students are doing, because in your case the play is neither safe nor enjoyable. A substitute must be found.

Obviously, the more rules and restrictions that either half of the team puts on their definitions of play and fun, the fewer options you will have. If you can run in circles with your dog for 10 minutes, allow your dog to leap onto your chest, and also wrestle on the ground, then you are very fortunate because you will have the widest range of options. But if you are in a wheelchair, your dog is an 80-pound rambunctious

Lab, and you have limited mobility of your upper body, then you will have the narrowest range of options. While this is unfortunate, it is also reality, so your best bet is to look long and hard at the games you CAN play: games of fetch using a soft ball in the house, hiding games, food games, and so on. Will these games be less fun for the dog? Possibly - but being realistic means we work with what we have and go from there.

Brenda and Buffy have found lots of ways to play, even with limited mobility. Find what works for you!

But My Dog Doesn't Like to Play!

What if your dog doesn't want any of things that you are offering, whether that's toys, food, or personal play? Well, simply put, you do not have a motivator if your dog does not want it; we certainly emphasized that in Book 2. Do not attempt to use something as a motivator in training until your dog shows a sustained interest in whatever you have to offer.

Trying harder won't work, so re-think your plan. If you've been physically wrestling with your dog and now you are seeing clear avoidance behaviors, adding even more pushing, pulling, and shoving certainly won't work. Remember, more of the same is a waste of time and often creates problems where there were none before. Our goal with this book is to help you find ways to play with your dog. We will encourage you to focus on learning the mechanical skills of play; often, developing these skills alone will open up a world of fun that you struggled to find before.

Unfortunately, we can't fix it all. Sometimes, you will need to let go of some of your emotions, hopes, and dreams for awhile. Let go of your frustration. Let go of your intensity. Let go of your determination to make your dog into something that he is not - or at least something he is not at this time.

The most poisonous part of motivation is a handler who cares too much about specific goals. Becoming process oriented is not something that we can teach you; it has to come from within. Letting go of rigid goals comes from an ability to realistically look at your team and learn to reach for the goals that are most fulfilling for both of you, not necessarily the ones you generated on your own. And paradoxically, this letting go is exactly what will allow your team to reach goals you may never have dreamed possible.

Denise's second Obedience Champion was a Belgian Tervuren named Cisu. Cisu started her competitive career with a long string of wins and high scores, and the future looked bright. As they began their quest for the OTCH title, though, something happened. Cisu began to get more and more stressed in the ring, and she started failing classes in which she had previously been a very consistent performer. Her failures made Denise more nervous and uncomfortable, and soon they were failing every trial consistently.

After taking a couple of years off to work with another dog and to regroup, Denise returned to the competition ring with Cisu. Because Cisu was already older and slowing down due to age, Denise gave up her goal of finishing Cisu's performance title and instead went back into competition with a new goal: to better understand her dog, to stay as connected as possible, and to become a true team.

That was all that Cisu needed. They finished their Obedience Championship with a string of wins in a matter of months. Only one thing changed: Denise had let go. When the title stopped being the driver of their time together, Team Cisu was able to shine.

The Moral of The Story Is...

We can give you techniques and ideas to foster your skills, but we cannot change what you feel in your heart. If you can reduce your personal pressure and enjoy the process of training, studying your dog, and finding what works and what does not work; if you can let go of the "recipes," the "have to's," and the rules that you have been told you must follow; if you can work with the dog you have – which is not necessarily the one you wanted – then your odds of success increase dramatically. You do not need to let go of your love of competition, but you do need to accept that dog sports are a team endeavor. Your focus needs to be on finding a way to encourage your dog to

*Work with what your dog loves.
Envy loves to play in water!*

become as passionate and comfortable with your sport as you are. Remember that you picked your sport; your dog had no say in the matter. Now your job is to show your dog, a tiny piece at a time, just how much fun it is to work with you in that sport.

And here comes the Catch 22: If you care a lot about which specific motivators your dog enjoys, it is very likely that you will add pressure to the game - not on purpose, but as a function of your underlying interest. It's the classic "oh please take this tug that I am stuffing into your face" problem. Rather than being fun, you begin to represent pressure to your dog, which will only make him avoid both you and the stimulus you are trying to force him to enjoy. You wanting it to be a motivator does not make it a motivator; motivation is internal to the individual. What you CAN do is learn excellent techniques of offering various motivators in ways that are likely to bring out your dog's natural interest in those things. The more you can squash your own desire to have your dog love food, toys, or personal play, the more likely it is that you will succeed in this regard.

Chapter Two
The Locus of Control

Giving our dogs the opportunity to make good choices while also respecting their needs and preferences is a central part of our training philosophy. We have discussed these concepts at length in our first two books, from the importance of building a cooperative relationship with our dogs to finding the best ways to motivate them to want to work with us. Now we need to find ways to build our dogs' drive and determination for those motivators, and we believe the best way to do this is through play.

Before we can get into the nuts and bolts of how to develop play in your dog, we need to discuss a new concept: the locus of control. The term "locus" refers to the place, location, or origination of something. Therefore, "the locus of control" can be interpreted to mean the source of control.

Many of the games we will introduce in this book will have an external locus of control; meaning that control comes from an outside source. You will hold your dog back or tease him with a specific motivator, such as a toy, ball, or cookie. This is intentional. When building up a dog's determination to get a specific motivator, we do not ask a dog to show self-control. Instead, we encourage him to fight for the motivator by implementing external control. There is a very strong relationship between where and how control is applied and the specific desire that is built into your dog, making the question of internal control versus external control important.

Zuzu's desire for the toy is being built through external control in the form of a harness and leash.

Is Internal Control or External Control Better?

Trainers often have very strong opinions on which locus of control should be emphasized. Trainers who have confident dogs with plenty of drive for motivators often choose to focus on internal control, especially if their dog has so much desire for a motivator that he can no longer think. On the other hand, trainers who have softer dogs often rely on external control; doing so helps build up hardness, determination, and self-confidence.

To understand how both forms of control work, let's say your dog wants a cookie that is on the floor. You do not want your dog to take the cookie just yet, so you place your dog on a stay, which he understands.

In this scenario, external forms of control might include the following: repeating the stay cue, applying leash pressure that prevents your dog from moving forward, or holding the dog back by the ruff or chest. All of these actions cause the dog to look for an opportunity to get around you. As soon as you release the pressure (by letting go of the collar, no longer repeating the command, stepping out of the way, etc.), your dog will spring towards the cookie. By applying external control, you have increased your dog's desire to escape from restraint to get what he wants.

Internal forms of control require you to control the environment instead of the dog. Examples might include placing your foot over the cookie if the dog moves out of his stay, placing the cookie out of reach on a table, using a helper to guard the cookie, and so on. In each case, the dog is allowed to do as he wishes, but you do not allow access to the cookie until the dog complies with your stay cue. Your dog learns by exploring the possible consequences, and discovers that self-restraint and cooperation with you is the best way to his goal.

Chewie is learning that the route to the cookie is through eye contact, not helping himself! He is developing an internal locus of control.

Ultimately, the locus of control is about whether or not your dog wants something. External controls are more appropriate for dogs who aren't so sure they even care. ("Ball? I don't want to chase a ball." This is a principle commonly referred to as reverse psychology.) As soon as you tell someone that they can't have something, it becomes much more valuable. Internal controls are more appropriate for dogs

Lola doesn't need more external control - she needs drive building for that ball!

Rafael really wants the toy! Now is the time to develop his internal locus of control.

who already love the motivator. ("Ball? I want that ball! What do I have to do to get it?") This encourages the dog to think and make decisions about what he needs to do in order to get what he already really wants.

In a nutshell, you should externally control the dog if your goal is to build drive and desire for a specific motivator, and require internal control if your goal is to create a more thoughtful dog. This is why choosing internal versus external control is not a matter of right and wrong. It is a matter of selecting the most appropriate training technique for your specific dog in any specific situation.

Training for Balance

Of course, choosing between internal control and external control is not as easy as matching it to the level of drive your dog has. The variables that influence training are fluid. The type of control you use will also depend on the age of your dog, the stage of training he is in, and your goals. It will also vary by motivator; if your dog loves cookies but could not care less about tug, then training for cookies should involve internal controls and training for tugs should involve external controls. And to complicate matters further, the exercise you are working on will also influence the type of control you use. If you want your dog to be calm, then focus on internal controls – they encourage your dog to think. But if you want your dog as intense as possible, then switching to external controls makes sense - at least for this particular exercise.

Choosing a particular locus of control is not a permanent decision. Within a given training session, you might find yourself switching back and forth, depending on what you wish to accomplish. There is one more consideration that needs to be introduced. We have talked about holding dogs back with external control to build drive, and we have talked about controlling the environment to develop self-control in dogs with well-developed drive. But the topic becomes truly fascinating where these two seemingly opposite forms of control intersect.

Once a dog wants something enough that you can use it in training, then asking for self-restraint will have the beneficial side effect of also developing drive. Here's how it works: when a dog desperately wants something, and when he recognizes that it will only happen if he controls himself, then every ounce of his being focuses on that object. When he is released, the energy that had been directed towards self-control is now directed towards the object as the dog springs towards it. This explosive release will build desire and drive while simultaneously building self-control - assuming, of course, that you only ask for what the dog can give in terms of both intensity (difficulty of your requests) and endurance (how long he must perform).

When done correctly, asking your dog for self-control builds drive.
Here, Bella is completely focused on the release.

If this has not been your experience - that is, if asking for self-control actually lowers your dog's drive - then one of two things has happened. Either your dog truly did not have sufficient drive to work on self-control in the first place (in which case you should go back to external controls in order to build that desire) or you asked your dog to exercise self-control in too difficult a fashion or for too long. In the latter case, your dog simply gave up on getting the desired object and settled into a lower arousal state as a result. It's always better to ask for extremely short duration (think a second or two) under high distraction than to ask a dog to sit in drive for a minute or more.

Here's a human example to make this clearer:

If you were about to run a race, you would come onto the track to "take your marks." Because you are old enough to have self-control, you would hold this position until you were told to go. But what would happen if there was a delay? You're standing there, ready to run, and the official in charge takes this time to tie his shoes, get a drink of water, and announce the results of the last race. More than likely, you'd begin to relax. If you were very young and impulsive, you might simply start running, but as a mature individual, you would reduce your internal drive - not because the activity isn't important, but because being on the edge of absolute focus and readiness is exhausting if the release does not come in a timely manner.

The ideal performance dog needs to be trained and handled to develop balance - tons of forward drive and determination, with exactly the right amount of self-control to create a "spring" effect. Creating that balance takes sophisticated and intelligent training that has been carefully designed for your dog's individual traits and needs at any given time. This is why cookie cutter training is often not successful. It cannot possibly take into account the enormous amount of variation in dogs at different times and for different activities.

Balance is created by observing your dog carefully and being flexible in your response. What your dog needs will be changing all of the time; recognizing this fact will allow

Balance requires a trainer that is flexible.
Ask yourself what makes sense for that training session.

you to instantly change your approach as required, depending on what your dog is telling you. What was appropriate last week may not be appropriate this week. And what was appropriate for one sport or one exercise may not be appropriate for another sport, or even on a different exercise within the same sport!

When training puppies and young dogs, we want to introduce both types of control early and often, but as we come to learn about the pup's behavior and personality, we will likely move towards one type of control training more often than another. That's fine as long as you remember that you may need to change your focus on a moment's notice. Don't get stuck believing your pup is high drive and therefore ALWAYS needs internal control work. That may be true for some activities and situations, but not for them all.

This can be difficult, so when in doubt, follow this simple rule of thumb: apply internal controls to dogs who are stronger and more confident, and external controls to softer and less sure dogs. If you still can't decide, prioritize drive and desire for work and start adding self-control exercises and games later.

Modifying Games to Meet Your Needs

Because this book is primarily about building drive and motivation, we will emphasize external controls. That said, most of the techniques and games we will describe can easily be modified to emphasize self restraint by changing the locus of control. This means that drive building games and self-control games are the same games, just with one small change between them.

Here's a simple example: the "Race to the Cookie" game from our upcoming food play chapter. In this game, a cookie is tossed straight ahead while the dog is held back by the ruff, collar, or chest (external control). The dog is then released and both the dog and handler take off, racing for the cookie!

In this exciting game, the dog is not required to show self-control - but we can modify it so that he is. Any time you introduce internal control to a game, start small. In this case, you will tell your dog to stay and PLACE the cookie on the floor (a food toss is much too exciting when you're introducing the game). Wait just long enough to be sure that your dog is staying (only a second or two), then release your dog with a race to the cookie! On subsequent repetitions, you can drop the cookie rather than setting it down, and slowly build up to a cookie toss. If your dog breaks his stay at any point, simply cover the cookie with your foot (or have a helper standing by to help with this). You can continue to increase the challenge by adding a position change or some work to the game before releasing your dog to the cookie. For example, ask your dog to switch from a sit to a down position before the release. If your dog breaks the stay, cheerfully remove the cookie (or use a helper) and start over. The key here is to do it cheerfully. Remember, your dog learns regardless of his choice - but only if you allow him the freedom to figure it out without interference. Do not attempt to stop him. Do not say no. Do not try to hold him back. Let him choose. Your dog will have to think very hard about holding that position until released, which will increase both self-control and handler focus. Just don't push too hard - you want him to win at least as often as he loses, and preferably a lot more than that!

Here, Kessie shows both internal and external control in the game "race for the cookie."

Kessie is held back.

They race for the cookie.

Kessie holds a stay.

Kessie explodes forward!

Can't get your dog to fail anymore? Try the above scenario, but instead of releasing to the cookie after the position change, begin to race to the cookie yourself without releasing your dog, but just for a few steps! Success leads to an immediate send and the dog gets the cookie. Failure leads to a cheerful reset to try again! Still can't get your dog to break? Instead of racing to the cookie, return to your dog and ask him to heel away a few steps before suddenly sending him for a race back to the cookie.

If your dog isn't very interested in the cookie, change your game plan and add external controls to build drive for those cookies as described in the upcoming chapters. Almost all of the food games can also be played with a toy instead, so to work on internal control, substitute a ball or something else your dog has plenty of drive for.

As you read, feel free to come up with your own options for each game. How might you and your dog enjoy them the most? What will be the most fun for you both? Which motivators would you like to see become stronger in your dog, and which motivators are ideal for creating more self-control?

As you can see, the sky's the limit in terms of options - just remember to keep balance at all times. Too many control games will weaken your dog's determination and self-confidence, especially if he loses frequently. Structure games so that your dog can succeed on most repetitions. If you've made it too hard, move on to something else and try again later with more reasonable expectations.

Ikon explodes out of work for his ball!

Conclusion

Done well, shifting to internal controls eventually strengthens the dog's drive rather than dampening it because the release becomes an explosion of power, focus, and intensity. Once your dog figures out how to win at the games you present, he will become an eager and enthusiastic participant. The trick is asking for exactly the right amount of control, which is the amount that the dog is able to give at that moment. You want your expectations to be challenging, not overly difficult for your dog. Making it too easy means that your dog doesn't improve, but making it too hard isn't fair and can lead to your dog giving up or being excessively frustrated. This exact right amount of challenge is a moving target, so you must continuously monitor your dog and be prepared to make changes on the fly!

Chapter Three
Mechanical Skills, Art and Play

At first glance, it might seem like the title of this chapter doesn't quite make sense. It's hard to see the connection between something as dry, boring, and technical as mechanical skills, and something as creative, intuitive, and fun as art or play. Despite the fact that they appear to be unrelated concepts, skillful training happens where they intersect.

The truth is, technical and precise physical abilities are necessary for artistic development. A good painter, for example, typically develops excellent technique through years of practice. A professional dancer spends endless hours practicing basic movements before she can put them together in creative routines. What's more, mechanical skills can actually increase enjoyment in play: most people find it more fun to play a recreational sport when they can do it almost effortlessly.

If you can master all three - mechanical skills, art, and play - then you are highly likely to be a very effective and efficient trainer. Some trainers are naturals; they grasp the general ideas and apply them without much conscious thought or effort - but that's rare. Most of us have to learn and practice (and then learn and practice some more) in order to become proficient.

This chapter will help you develop all three. We'll talk about some of the basic mechanical skills that are needed for all forms of play. We will also encourage you to be spontaneous and flexible so that you can develop intuition about what your dog needs at any given time - in other words, the art of training. And then you'll want to get out there and play, play, play!

What are Mechanical Skills?

In dog training, when we talk about mechanical skills, we mean physically responding in a quick and appropriate way. For example, if you are in a shaping session, then excellent mechanical skills would presume that you are marking behaviors at exactly the right instant, rewarding in the correct position, and

Justice and Tamandra have learned great play together!

raising criteria appropriately. As a result, your dog is able to progress quickly with low levels of stress. Excellent mechanical skills are normally acquired as a trainer gains hands-on experience working with dogs.

Olga gently pressures Spark, and he responds with enthusiasm!

Major mechanical skills in dog training include observation, timing, setting and raising criteria, and reinforcement delivery. These skills apply to teaching behaviors as well as to playful interactions. There is no fundamental difference between good training and good play. The underlying foundations are the same, and therefore, the mechanical skills are the same. It's important to carefully observe your dog as you try to initiate play and change your actions based on his responses. Is moving towards him with frontal pressure causing a curious reaction, or is he moving away and looking concerned? In that split second, you need to be able to see and respond to your dog's behavior. If your timing is off - maybe you haven't waited quite long enough for your dog to process your actions and respond - you will seem overwhelming and either send your dog into avoidance or cause a defensive response.

Knowing when and how to move in and apply pressure and when to move away to relieve pressure comes from a combination of mechanical skills, which we will discuss in depth in this chapter. Remember, in play, the entire interaction is the reinforcer, and our job is to make sure that it is exactly that. If our dogs ever indicate in any small way that they are not thoroughly enjoying the interaction, then we need to change something immediately.

Perfect Practice Makes Perfect

To be useful, mechanical skills must be practiced until they become second nature. Initially, mechanical skills require conscious thought to apply, and when you are actively thinking about what you are doing, you don't have the ability to totally immerse yourself in the activity. While there is no substitute for practice, not just any practice will do. You need PERFECT practice. Practicing something incorrectly for twenty years doesn't make you a better trainer, it just makes it nearly impossible for you to change your technique.

Once past the initial learning phase, it is highly likely that your mechanical skills will drift and alter over time. This tendency for behavior to change is good when we are training our dogs because it allows us to make small, precise changes. However, it also means that we must work hard to maintain perfect behaviors, both in ourselves and our dogs.

Professional athletes have coaches because it is very difficult to maintain perfect practice without consistent feedback on their performance. If you cannot afford a professional coach, there are other options to keep your mechanical skills in shape. Our favorite is to use a video camera. It's amazing how great a difference there is between what we think we do and what we actually do, and without videotape, you have no way of knowing the difference. Reviewing video recordings with an objective and critical eye is one of the most valuable training tools you can use. If you are a less experienced trainer, finding a more experienced mentor or teacher who will review your videotapes with you is a HUGE advantage. Over time you will learn to evaluate your own tapes with a critical and discerning eye.

Those who attend competitions with their dogs often have someone videotape their performances. This serves not only as a visual memory for the event, but also as an opportunity to compare perception to reality. Often, the way a performance feels

Get in the habit of videotaping your training!

Videotape your competitions; they might look very different than they felt!

differs from the way it actually looks. It's important to note these instances and try to reconcile them. For example, Deb had a recent run in the rally ring with Star, her young Border Collie, that felt very disconnected and awkward. In fact, it felt like a complete disaster! But the videotape told a different story. While Star was not as intensely focused as she normally is, she was still performing the trained skills quite well. Reviewing the video helped Deb pinpoint the exact moment the disconnect occurred, which gave her valuable information for future training.

Having a group to train with offers the opportunity for feedback on your work!

Having a training partner or a group of training buddies can be helpful as well, especially if they give kind and thoughtful feedback. This is most helpful from someone who has the same basic training background and approach as you do. Well-meaning folks are usually happy to give advice, but that's not what we want; we want informed and educated feedback, and not everyone is capable of giving us that.

Either way, the goal of videotaping or having someone observe your training sessions is to identify areas for improvement, as well as to note areas of success. Getting accurate and precise feedback will definitely help you improve your mechanical skills.

The Intersection of Skill and Art

The mechanical skills of play can and should be mastered through study, but to a certain extent, it is impossible to totally separate them from intuition. You probably already use the mechanical skills we're going to discuss when interacting playfully with other people, and with a bit of thought we can adapt them to our canine play partners.

If you pay attention, you'll quickly learn what forms of play work best for your dog.
Bella loves her bumper!

The most important thing you can do when playing is to pay attention: what is your dog's response to your attempts at engagement? How do these responses vary from dog to dog? Can you identify any commonalities that will help you engage your next play partner more quickly?

Here's an example: Denise plays with a lot of dogs and has learned that using the opposition reflex, where she gently pushes on a dog and then springs away quickly, is often a powerful way to start a play session. Knowing just where and how hard to push on the dog is a mechanical skill that she has learned. But through experience, Denise has also learned that this technique works much better with dogs who are familiar with her as a play partner. As a result, she uses this technique with great care when engaging a new dog for the first time, and she has found ways to use more subtle forms of this technique until the dog's behavior suggests that it might okay to try opposition reflex in a play session. In this manner, the mechanical skill of engaging play through opposition reflex combines with the art of training.

Opposition reflex can be extremely effective for developing play - but you have to know when the dog is ready. Megan and Gus are having a great time with this play based skill.

Flow

Flow is a mental, emotional, and physical state of total immersion in an engaging activity. This concept has been discussed and researched in the psychological literature and popularized by a researcher named Mihaly Csikszentmihalyi, but most of us have probably experienced flow without ever knowing what it is called. If you have ever been so involved in something that you didn't notice time passing and were surprised when you discovered how long you'd been engaged in it, then you have experienced flow.

Many people seek out hobbies precisely for this experience. They want an activity that is totally engaging because it makes for a wonderful break from day to day concerns and worries. When in flow, the mind is intensely focused on a task - but it is an enjoyable and rewarding task!

Our goal for play sessions is that both human and dog will experience flow throughout the interaction. This requires both parties to be totally focused on and completely enjoying the activity. This doesn't mean that the interaction has to be easy or highly arousing - flow can occur when working on challenging tasks that require concentration as well as when working on less demanding ones - it simply means that there is mutual voluntary engagement and enjoyment.

Three Factors Affecting Play

There are three general factors that should be considered regardless of the specific play technique you are using. Mastering an understanding of intensity, proximity, and duration will make you much more successful in engaging a dog. If you read the last book, these terms should sound familiar, but they are so important that we're going to briefly revisit them here.

1. Intensity

Intensity is hard to define when discussing play because intensity is about personal pressure, energy, and presence, which always changes depending on the players. One person's definition of intense might be perceived as relatively mild by another person.

The ability to capture the attention of another being through subtle qualities such as posture, stance, eye contact, stillness, and so on, are all functions of intensity. An intense person can overwhelm another person who is much larger or more physically imposing. Qualities that affect intensity include movement (direction of travel, speed, quick changes), size (larger, looming, smaller, retreating), eye contact (hard or soft), and body posture (tense or relaxed, open hands or fists).

Each person has a degree of intensity that he or she will bring to a play session. The trick is not to change it, but rather to judge how it is affecting your partner. In some cases, raising your intensity will be just the ticket for catching your dog's eye and starting an excellent play session, while in another situation or with a different dog, the correct answer will be ratcheting your intensity down, possibly even becoming as non-threatening or as low intensity as possible.

This protection helper is showing extreme intensity, and the dog is responding with equal intensity!

More intensity is NOT the answer when play is not going well. The goal is to match your partner, not to overwhelm him. For example, when an adult wishes to engage with a child, most of us will naturally identify where the child is in terms of energy and mental engagement, and then meet him or her at that place. Adults recognize that we have position power, so we work hard to avoid frightening children.

The same should be true with dogs! Too much intensity is both frightening and stressful for a dog. Softer, more sensitive dogs avoid hyper-intense people - and a dog in handler avoidance is a trainer's worst nightmare! The reverse is also true; lively, quick dogs are bored by people who lack sufficient intensity to capture their attention, and they will leave and find other ways to entertain themselves.

If you're struggling to find the right level of intensity, try using a number system. How much intensity is your dog giving at the moment? A bright-eyed dog bouncing around and engaging you with play bows and barking may well be up at a nine or a ten. You're going to have to be ready to give a lot of energy and intensity back if you want to play with him! Standing quietly and inviting a belly rub isn't going to cut it. Why not try an eight?

Maddie is lively so a higher level of intensity might be appropriate!

Today Kip is calm, so a quiet demeanor is perfect for Kip's young handler.

But what if your dog is standing quietly, just barely wagging his tail in your presence? Then running, whooping, and grabbing his feet is likely to put him into active handler avoidance. This dog is offering a two or three out of ten, while you're going all out! How about scaling back your intensity to a three and see how that works for you?

If you want your dog be more intense, start where he is and add one notch. If your dog is offering a two and you want a five, try a three and see if you can work yourself to a higher level of intensity over several sessions. On the other hand, if your dog is too wound up, offering a nine when you'd like to see a five, try giving an eight and work your way down over time. If you start at a one, you won't even show up on your dog's radar. You have to get his attention and then bring him to where you are, one bit at a time.

Being able to move your dog into different levels of arousal depending on the activity is critical. A dog at an arousal level of ten might be perfect for an agility trial, but a three is probably better for a dog just learning how to work a pile of scent articles. Practice varying your intensity level and see how that leads to changes in your dog.

2. Proximity

Proximity refers to how physically close you are to your dog. As a general rule, being very close to another creature increases stress and pressure, especially when you are involved in an energetic activity like play. If your dog appears a bit nervous about your play, try changing your proximity. For example, if your dog is on one side of a table and you are on the other side, running back and forth, you are much less likely to be perceived as a threat than if you are both on the same side of the table. The same is true if you are playing tag with your dog. The closer you are to tagging your dog, the more intense the situation will be, and the higher the risk for frightening your dog rather than engaging in play. Try giving your dog more space and see if that helps the overall play dynamic. If your dog seems bored by your play, try moving closer to your dog - maybe even grabbing him! Any activity that involves hands on play, whether touching your dog while playing tug or wrestling on the floor, will increase proximity. This is neither good nor bad, but if you'd like to change the tone of your play, take a moment to consider your proximity.

Raika is comfortable in close proximity with her handler but not necessarily with other people.

The speed with which you change your proximity can be a huge factor in your dog's response. If you quickly rush towards your dog without warning, you are probably going to startle him, not engage him. On the other hand, slow and quiet movement might be totally ignored, so you need to find the middle ground where your dog will both notice your movement and be intrigued by it.

Some dogs have larger personal space preferences than others. And some dogs have no need for personal space at all! This is often a breed tendency. For example, most Labrador Retrievers are notoriously clueless regarding body space, while many smaller dogs are highly sensitive to someone coming too close. This does vary between each individual dog, so the best rule of thumb is to observe the dog to determine his personal space needs before you try to engage him.

Kip doesn't mind being hugged, but Sin's body language suggests she needs more personal space.

3. Duration

When it comes to play, less is more. It is ALWAYS preferable to end a session before the dog is ready for it to end. Pushing for just a bit longer often backfires. If your dog disengages before you are ready to stop, then you made a mistake. When you go into a play session, you need to have a good idea of how long the session will last. If you just play until it's over, you are likely to go on for way too long. If you do want to play for a somewhat longer period of time then make a point of inserting short breaks into your play sessions to allow both of you to regroup.

Also, keep in mind that many forms of play are taxing for the dog. Chasing a ball across a field for ten minutes might not seem like a lot, but you're not the one running up and down the field! Some dogs will lose steam, both mentally and physically, very quickly. You can build up their stamina for play over time with slight increases in duration over the course of a

Playing ball is hard work for highly driven dogs like Duzi and Vudoo!

number of sessions. But even if a dog is willing to play until he drops, that doesn't mean it's good for him. Some dogs become mentally exhausted but physically keep going. We want to help these dogs sync their mental and physical efforts over time. Games that require concentration and thought will need to be increased slowly and carefully, while simple physical play can go on for much longer.

Conclusion

As you work your way through this book, take some time to think about how mechanical skills and art intersect. You will also want to keep the factors of intensity, proximity, and duration in mind. As you read, ask yourself how these factors might play out with a specific move or skill. If it's a technical skill that requires a very specific posture or movement, consider mastering that skill without your dog present first. When you feel comfortable with it, add the dog to the game. If you work hard to improve your skills, it is highly likely that your dog will respond favorably to your efforts.

Chapter Four
Introduction to Tug Games

Working bred dogs can be extremely persistent tuggers.

Few topics have created more argument, confusion, and anxiety between trainers than discussions of playing tug with their performance dogs. It is hard to overstate what a good game of tug can do in terms of increasing your dog's enthusiasm, energy, and joy - all of which can be used to motivate and refine performance work. Dogs bred from working lines or for working sports can be very powerful and persistent in their games of tug, and it is no coincidence that these dogs make up a high percentage of the top performance dogs in IPO (protection work), agility, and obedience.

On the other hand, there are dogs who are low in innate toy interest, or who are simply lower energy dogs altogether. Sometimes trainers who have limited experience with these less-driven dogs are highly judgmental of those teams that have not learned to play. These trainers seem to suggest that if the dog cannot play, the owner is at fault because she simply hasn't tried hard enough to make her dog play. Furthermore, the implication is that the dog cannot succeed in performance competition without the ability to play tug, increasing pressure on the owner to make it happen.

As we discussed in the second book in this series, if you MAKE your dog do something that he doesn't really want to do, you'll have exactly the opposite effect of what was intended. Best-case scenario: the dog learns to find joy in the game in spite of the methods used to teach it. Worst-case scenario: the dog develops anxiety at the sight of the trainer or a toy. Regardless, there is simply no reason to approach any activity involving your dog with this type of pre-existing pressure. Rarely does a stressed-out and pressured trainer produce a confident and happily playing dog.

Non-traditional breeds can also love tug, but sometimes the game has to be introduced with more thought and care.

Pip loves to tug and she also releases without conflict, making the game a great way to build energy into their training interactions!

A trainer can deprive a dog of normal life pleasures like social interaction in an effort to force toy interest - and sometimes this works. But before you take this route, ask yourself how much you are willing to deprive your dog in order to create more interest in playing with you. Do not mindlessly add more deprivation when your toy play isn't generating the desired results. You may be able to teach a dog to play using intense deprivation, but dogs trained this way rarely bring true joy to the picture. Instead, this method of teaching can lead to frantic play, which has more to do with avoiding the deprivation than loving the activity. Mild deprivation is not of great concern, but please think twice before subjecting your dog to weeks, months, or a lifetime of crating or social deprivation in an attempt to artificially create an interest in working with you.

Thankfully, it is quite possible to teach a dog to play tug without deprivation, and we are going to lay out a systematic plan over the next few chapters about how to do so. Before we do that, though, we need to take some time to consider what tug is and why it's worth putting in the time to develop the mechanical skills needed to play tug well.

So What is Tug?

When we talk about tug, we are specifically talking about the interactive game created when a handler teases a dog with an object, encouraging him to chase and grab it. The game is about interacting with one another, not winning or losing. The game has its greatest versatility when the sight of a toy and a cue such as "get it!" causes the dog to immediately grab hold of the offered object and play with the trainer. When the trainer asks the dog to release, the ideal picture includes a dog who immediately releases the toy without conflict, ready to return to play or work as directed.

Conflict

The goal of tug is interactive play. Unfortunately, tug can result in conflict, which exists when the interests of the dog and the interests of the trainer are at odds with each other. For example, if the dog wants to play with a tug toy that is sitting on the training field, and the handler wants the dog to perform an agility obstacle, the result will be conflict for the dog. He must choose between obeying his trainer and running for the toy.

When teaching your dog to tug, the goal is to avoid conflict. This is accomplished by helping the dog understand that he can have it both ways. If he obeys his trainer's cues, then not only will he get to have the toy, but his trainer will also actively engage with him and the toy. This is much more satisfying than simply holding an unmoving tug toy. Avoiding conflict in this way not only satisfies each party's interests, but actually strengthens them. The trainer gets the obstacle performed at top speed because the dog is excited about the pending reward. The dog gets the toy and a terrific game with the trainer.

It is your job as a trainer to show your dog why it is in his best interest to cooperate with you. Everything you teach, from the most basic play skills to the most complex exercises, must be taught with the goal of avoiding conflict whenever possible –

Crna has learned that heeling earns a toy reward. There is no stress or conflict here, even though her handler is holding a toy while they work.

which should be the vast majority of the time. We will discuss this at length in this book, but you may also wish to review the chapter on focus from the first book.

The Relationship Between Drives and Tug

In our experience, dogs who play very easily tend to be dogs with strong working drives, while dogs who come from breeds designed to be quiet family companions or more independent workers tend to bring less innate toy interest to the table. Some dogs are just easier to play with because the game is inherently valuable for them. Despite this, how far each team will be able to take their toy play is highly individual. Trainers who have good skills but have to work extremely hard to make toys important to their dogs start with a handicap because the dog's innate interests are lower. On the other hand, trainers who lack the mechanical skills to make tug a rewarding activity for their dogs will struggle to make interactive toy play fun, regardless of how much their dogs might want to play.

Most of the dogs who compete in AKC performance events fall somewhere in the middle in terms of drive to play. Their trainers often believe the dogs cannot or will not play, but these dogs WILL play if the game is presented to them in a positive and interactive manner by a trainer with good mechanical skills. They have the genetic capacity to play and to truly enjoy the game, but they require some help to recognize how much fun it can be. A trainer who understands the subtleties of play, or who is naturally inclined toward it, can often bring this playfulness to the surface where it can significantly enhance time spent working or training together.

While these middle of the road dogs don't always express the intensity and commitment shown by natural players, many of them WILL develop a love of toy play that can surpass their interest in food as a motivator. This alone makes interactive toy play a game worthy of attention. Even if a dog does not reach this level of commitment, there is still significant value to toy play as an addition to food in training, which makes it well worth the effort.

Good tug play is both a mechanical skill and an art. Good tug is also an emotional and interactive skill. If you do not make a point of investing yourself in the game, then you will lose the benefits of the relationship building aspects of toy play. If a dog loves to play tug, either by nature or through positive exposures over time, he will begin to associate you with this fabulous game. This adds value to your smile, movements, and personal interactions with your dog. This side effect of classically conditioning YOU with the fun of the game is huge, especially if you plan to compete in sports where you will not have access to your external motivators for long periods of time, or where your dog will eventually figure out that classic rewards will never show up in competition.

The Benefits of Tug

There are many reasons why we play tug. This section will consider several specific benefits.

Energy

Most dogs generate a good deal of physical energy when they play tug. They engage their bodies from nose to tail, pulling downwards or pushing in, holding on with their feet and shaking their heads from side to side. Unlike the mindless energy of a dog zooming around madly with no focal point, this energy is very much focused on the game. As a result, the energy created by playing tug is available for performance activities once the dog is asked to release the toy. Dogs, like humans, tend to stay amped up after they do something physical, and we want to harness this energy to fuel our work together.

Playing tug with Buffy creates energy, which she channels into her work!

Speed

Dogs working for a game of tug are already in a mode that expresses physical energy; a dog excited by the game can't wait to engage! Because an energized dog naturally performs faster, systematically raising criteria for what earns a game of tug can teach a dog to respond to your cues immediately. Speed can then become a condition for earning a toy. Drop quickly on a down command? Finish that dog walk in record time? Perform out-of-motion exercises instantly? That earns a game of tug!

Great games of tug create great speed! Rafael is running out of the chute and straight towards his tug!

Endurance

Dogs working for the promise of a toy tend to work energetically for much longer stretches of time than dogs working for food rewards. This is particularly true when the dog must exhibit self-control. Dogs actively controlling themselves in the hopes of toy play tend to become highly engaged in the activity rather than being passive recipients of information. This is especially important when the work is not inherently interesting, like precision heeling, mastering straight fronts, or holding contacts.

Toys can bridge the gap between the food used to improve one's precision and the energy desired for speed, especially over a longer training session. Any time there is a possibility that the work will suck energy out of the dog, release to a toy is often preferred - even if food is used to reward specific behaviors before the big reward. After a toy release, many dogs will happily participate in another round of drills. Once the dog has received a toy play reward, you have the additional benefit of a dog in a higher state of arousal, which brings more energy into subsequent training sessions. This leads to a positive cycle of energy - to work - to more energy.

Ring Sport competition dogs are on the field for up to thirty minutes; they will work that long for a chance to bite (play tug) with the decoy.

Focus

In addition to physical energy, speed, and endurance, tug uses targeted mental energy, otherwise known as focus. Focus is also expressed as energy, speed, and endurance, but instead of a physical manifestation of these traits, it is expressed through concentration and learning. As we have discussed previously, focused dogs are easier to train and are attentive, bright, cheerful learners.

To successfully apply games of tug to increase focus, the trainer must challenge the dog at exactly his level of ability. Dogs quickly learn that they must pay attention or they could lose their toys. For example, if a dog is playing tug and is then mildly distracted by a bird flying overhead, the dog is likely to pause and forget to bite down for a second or two. A skilled trainer takes that opportunity to gleefully snag the toy away and enjoy a few seconds of victory. The next time a bird flies overhead, the dog clamps down more firmly with a "you can't fool me!" attitude. In the same vein, a dog who is almost distracted in the middle of a learning task - but then remembers that he is working for the promise of a toy reward - will pull himself back to the game, creating an internal desire to learn which is expressed as focus.

Halo shows extreme focus at this flyball competition because he wants his tug at the end!

With time, the focus developed during play is equaled by the focus offered by the dog trying to earn that toy in work – another positive cycle. Focus improves the likelihood of receiving a toy, and the toy reward leads to better focus. It's a win-win situation for both the dog and the trainer!

Developing a Working Relationship

One of the most valuable aspects of playing tug with your dog is what it does for your relationship. It is extremely difficult to play well with a dog unless you can accurately read your dog's emotional state at any given moment. If you play with your dog regularly, then you will know what is normal for your dog. You know how quickly your dog engages, how hard he bites down, and how strongly he interacts with you. If you find that your dog is significantly different than normal in a new environment – either by the amount of bite pressure you feel on the toy or by the lessened engagement you sense - then you can make smart choices about how to proceed. People who regularly play with their dogs tend to become experts in their dogs' behavior.

Another highly valuable aspect of interactive toy play is the 100% focus and engagement that a tug game requires from the trainer. It is extremely difficult to play tug without immersing yourself fully in the game. As a general rule, people who play tug with their dogs focus on the dog – not on listening to other people talk or hanging out with their friends in the training building. Good tug demands that both parties be equally engaged, which promotes a better relationship.

Playing tug as a reward will have a positive effect on this team's working relationship.

Fun!

Finally, tug is FUN! It's fun to see your dog's bright eyes and happy face! You are giving your dog a game that he loves, and in turn, this game does wonders for your personal relationship. In particular, if you have to work hard to find the best route to your dog's heart, you will know your dog much better than a person with a dog who was born loving to play. Overcoming the challenge of a dog who doesn't play is highly gratifying, especially if you manage to do it in a manner that maintains the joy, spontaneity, and fun that tug is supposed to be.

This simple game offers more than exercise or a training reward; it offers FUN for everyone!

Conclusion

The next few chapters will move into the nitty gritty, nuts and bolts, how-to of developing your game of tug. As you move forward, remember that great tug is both a mechanical skill and an art - master both and you will love training and playing with your dog. And he will love training and playing with you!

No matter how excited you might be about the potential that toys can bring to a training program, before we go any further we need to discuss selecting the right type of toy. This will vary based on the dog and the situation. This chapter will discuss the different types of toys and when each one is most appropriate so you can make educated decisions about what might be best for your dog instead of adopting a trial-and-error approach.

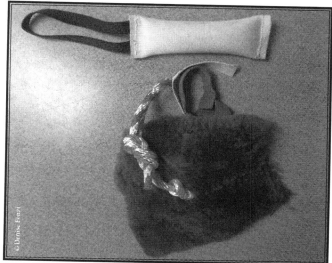

Which one is a better choice for your dog?

Why Toy Selection Matters

Understanding which toys to use and why is critical. Many dogs will play tug only if the right toy is used during each stage of the dog's training development. Many trainers have proclaimed that their dogs lack tug drive, when in reality, the dogs simply need different toys - and quite possibly a different presentation of that toy.

As a general rule, the younger your dog is when you start playing games with him, the easier your task will be because young puppies tend to be easily engaged by prey motion. If your puppy comes home at eight weeks, get started! Once teething starts, his mouth may be sore and you'll need to

Young puppies tend to do better with soft, long, whippy toys.

be a bit careful about how you play. You may need to stop tug games entirely for a few weeks until he appears more comfortable. If you have already set a good foundation of play, the skill will not be lost with a short break. By six months of age, almost all dogs are ready to resume tug play. If you own one of those dogs who appear oblivious to teething discomfort, you can go ahead and play right through the teething period.

Age is pretty much irrelevant to selection of toys or to the progression of teaching play. As a result, we will use the terms "dog," "puppy," and "player" interchangeably throughout the rest of this chapter. Keep in mind that this chapter is about toy selection; specific instructions on how to use the toys will be explained in the following chapters.

Toys for Building Drive

Dogs with low prey drive, or a lack of experience with chasing toys as prey, need to have this interest built. In this context, prey drive is about a dog's reaction to any fast moving object, which is not necessarily live prey. A dog with good prey drive is easily attracted to a moving object and pays careful attention to its trajectory. If the object continues to move, the movement captures and maintains the dog's intense interest.

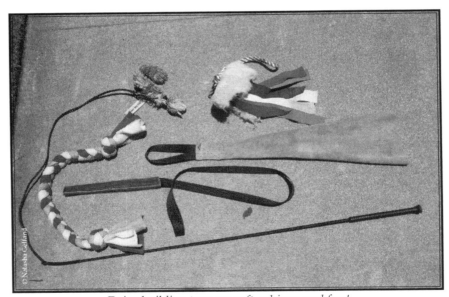

Drive building toys are soft, whippy and fun!

Drive-building toys are necessary to help a dog develop prey drive. These toys are long, lightweight, flexible in construction (as opposed to stiff), and easy for the handler to manipulate in an interesting fashion. We refer to these toys as "whippy" due to the quick and erratic movements they can make. Because the end goal for most handlers is for the dog to bite the toy, a drive-building toy should, generally, be made of a thin material that is easy to grab.

Examples of toys used to incite prey drive are:

1. Soft fleece toys with pieces hanging down that are easy to grab. Octopus and spider shapes work well.

2. "Puppy rags" made of chamois type or jute material and that is at least 18" long. The leather version is particularly valuable for dogs who need to learn to bite hard (IPO or protection dogs). The jute puppy rags are fine for all novice players.

Rabbit fur and real wool are popular drive building toys.

3. Toys with real fur. Some dogs go crazy for real fur but not for the fake versions. Rabbit is the most commonly available, but other options exist. Look for a piece that is strong enough to hold up to some use, but not so reinforced that it is stiff or lacks whippiness.

4. Flexible fur toys made with a pouch for food inside. Most of the time we find that the addition of food is a distraction instead of a benefit, however, it may be worth a try with dogs who don't respond to other options.

As you can see, basically any toy with a textured exterior surface that is easy to grab and has plenty of length to create fast and intense action is a good choice. Avoid toys that are short or stiff. These toys are NOT appropriate for novice players because their construction makes them difficult to use in a whippy fashion. In addition, they don't allow a novice dog to easily catch it and bite down with a strong grip. You should also avoid toys with smooth outer bite surfaces, such as synthetic toys made of slick fire hose rubber, both because they're too difficult for a young dog to bite and because they lack the desired flexibility.

If your dog has low confidence or is easily intimidated, he'll need to work further away from you on the softest possible bite surface you can find. You'll want a long toy you can throw away from your body. The surface should be very easy to grip; a soft toy with a lot of squish in the dog's mouth is ideal.

Toys for Training

Once your dog has completed the drive-building phase, you will need to introduce training toys. Unlike the soft, whippy drive-building toys, training toys are shorter and have a stiffer construction. It's important that you don't switch to a training toy until your dog is ready for it. We'll discuss this in more depth later on, but basically, you will know it is time to switch to a training toy when your dog no longer requires prey motion to incite him to play; as soon as you pull out your toy he attempts to grab it and play with you.

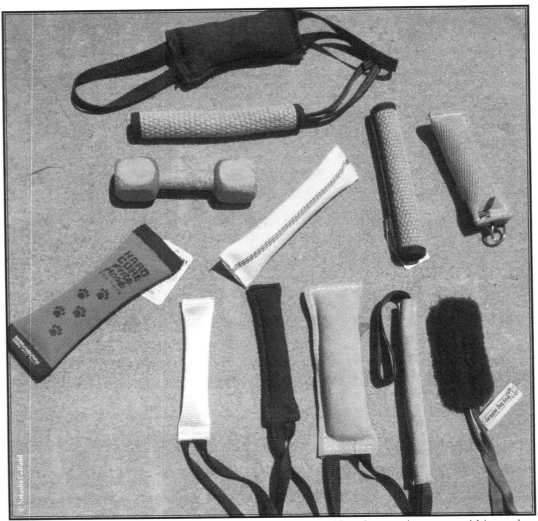

Training toys are likely to be shorter, stiffer, and harder, making them easier to use within work.

There are several advantages to moving your dog onto training toys as opposed to keeping him on drive building toys. First, training toys are much easier to offer while standing; you simply present the toy with one or two hands. Training toys make it obvious to the dog where he should bite, which makes the incidence of accidental hand bites much lower. Training toys are also easy to carry in a pocket, and playing with them does not tend to distract the other dogs around you. Finally, the stiffness of training toys makes it easier to get a dog to release without conflict. We'll discuss the release in great detail in an upcoming chapter.

Training Toys for Hard Biters

Dogs with very hard bites should be using a hard toy with a hard inner core, especially if the dog tends to thrash his head side to side while you're trying to hang on for dear life. With these dogs, look for toys designed for IPO dogs; they are often made out of materials such as hard leather, jute, or synthetic materials. They typically have wide diameter biting surfaces and harder interior fillings. Rather than the fluffy white stuff that we normally see inside of toys, hard toys may be rolled without any filling at all. As a bonus, toys for hard-biting dogs tend to hold up reasonably well over the long run.

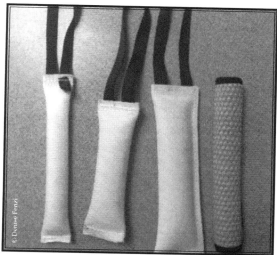

Toys made of rolled jute, leather and synthetic firehose are popular options for hard biting dogs.

Training Toys for Soft Biters

If your dog has a soft bite but a great desire to play, look for a toy with a softer and well textured exterior and a soft fill. You might want to find a toy with fur or fleece on the outside, but a stiffer construction on the inside. If your dog has a soft bite and minimal desire to play, you need to continue working with drive-building toys until the desire to play has increased.

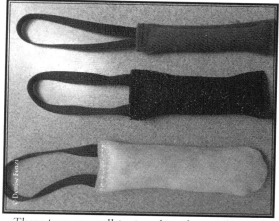

These toys are well textured on the outside and stuffed very softly (you can bend them in half), making them a good training toy for softer biters.

Conclusion

Choosing the right toy will make a huge difference in terms of your ability to play tug with your dog. Long, whippy toys are more motivating than short toys when used to incite a prey reaction. Use them for drive-building. Toys with more structure are better suited for training, and can be customized based on your dog's bite style.   When it comes right down to it, use what you and your dog find to be most comfortable and effective for both of you. Hopefully this chapter gave you some ideas for starting out.

In the next chapter, we will discuss how to build drive for tug, so get out your long, whippy toys!

Chapter Six
Building Tug Drive

It's never too early to start toy play!

Now that you have a drive-building toy, it's time to start building some awesome drive. This chapter will help you take your dog from uninterested or unenthusiastic to a dedicated tugger! Teaching a dog to tug is a matter of developing his prey drive. While some dogs are naturally higher in prey drive, most dogs can learn to tug - if you know how to teach them! And the best way to do this is to begin by asking yourself one question:

What would the squirrel do?

Picture this: there is a squirrel sitting on a fence. Your dog notices the squirrel, looks intently at it, and then starts moving towards it. The squirrel runs away! Even though your dog didn't catch the squirrel - he probably didn't even get within 50 feet of it - his interest has been piqued. The next time your dog sees the squirrel, there will be an additional edge of curiosity and boldness. He will probably move towards the squirrel much more

quickly – possibly with focused intent. Again, the squirrel runs away!

Even though the squirrel escaped, that does not dampen your dog's interest in catching him. Indeed, it will only further incite his prey drive. Each time your dog sees that squirrel, he gathers information. He learns how fast squirrels can run, what direction of travel they prefer, and what causes them to panic. These experiences will build his confidence, improve his visual tracking, and increase his determination to catch the squirrel – or at least to get much closer to it.

A large part of prey drive is visual tracking; getting the prey is not necessary in order to increase the dog's interest, focus, drive, and energy. It is critical to understand this because the biggest mistake trainers make when trying to teach their dogs to tug is trying so hard to get their dog to grab and hold the toy that they become overbearing.

Squirrels are NOT suicidal. Squirrels do not move towards the dog except in a momentary panic. Squirrels don't subject themselves to a thorough sniffing. Squirrels do not stand sideways in front of a dog, hoping to be bitten. And they certainly DON'T leap into the dog's mouth as the dog tries to get away!

Here, Risa is chasing a lure. Note the extreme speed, focus and energy which is typical of pure prey drive.

Kiyo is chasing an escaping squirrel!

The reality is that squirrels are highly frightened of dogs and their behavior reflects this: they run away and try to escape. Over time, an experienced squirrel might become bolder around dogs – waiting longer to run away if he has learned that the dog is unable to reach him - but this comes well after the dog is already throwing himself at the critter at every opportunity. This is the beginning of the chase.

First, Develop Your Skills

By now, you know that we think having good mechanical skills is essential to being a good play partner. To that end, you're going to learn how to play without your dog before involving him in the game; don't forget to videotape your session so you can evaluate your progress! Visualize your dog and what he might do! Without video, you will have to guess about the causes of any possible problems that might crop up.

Begin outside where you have some room to maneuver. Attach your drive-building toy to a lunge whip (these are available online or from a feed store). Move the lunge whip/toy combination in an erratic, squirrel-like fashion - remember, that means AWAY from your imaginary puppy. Because squirrels don't fly, keep the toy on the ground most of the time with only the occasional jump into the air.

Keep the toy moving AWAY from your imaginary dog.

You will want to practice until you can consistently control the lunge whip. You should become proficient at moving the toy at different speeds and in erratic changes of directions. Also, move your body as well as the toy. Practice handling the toy so that it is between you and your dog so that you're facing each other, and also so that it's parallel to your side. A parallel approach will be helpful if your puppy finds the game intimidating or if you are in a long and narrow area. The way you move the toy will depend on your puppy's reaction, so practice all of your options. A final note: get in the habit of keeping your hands and arms relatively close to your body when possible. This will help you when we move to more advanced work.

Now, go watch the videotape. Does your toy remind you of a squirrel? Do you feel comfortable changing directions if you get into the corner of your training area? Can you manage the toy when your imaginary puppy is facing different directions? If so, good! Go get your puppy. If not, study your video until you can pinpoint your errors. Too much time in the air? Too slow? Straight lines? Too aggressive? Work on it until you are satisfied that your play style is unpredictable, fun, and interesting. Be the squirrel!

Practice with the toy at different angles.

Parallel to your dog.

Facing each other as you back up.

With the dog between you and the toy.

Before You Start

Now that you have some squirrel-like technique, allow your puppy to watch you play from a window or a crate. You should notice A LOT of sustained interest coming from his direction. If your dog has had unsuccessful interactions with a toy in the past, feel free to stay at this stage for several sessions. Make sure your dog is convinced you're having fun! Add sound effects like laughing, squealing, and squeaking! Act like playing with this toy is the highlight of your day! Try to avoid looking directly at your crated puppy to gauge his reaction; use your peripheral vision.

If you already have another dog that plays, feel free to allow the puppy to watch while you further refine your technique on your current player. Most dogs find chasing toys on lunge lines extremely entertaining even if they've been playing tug for years, and watching another dog play can be just the ticket for a puppy who is observing from a crate.

Now go watch your video. Do you look inviting or intimidating? Did you remember to focus on the toy and not on the puppy in the crate? Is your puppy whining, barking, crying, or staring intently at you and your toy? If so, great! You are ready for the next step.

Puppy, Meet Squirrel

When your pup enters the picture, you'll want to choose your location well. Avoid areas with lots of interesting smells or sights - this is not the time to try and compete with the real squirrels running in your trees. Make sure there are no children or other dogs present to discourage, intimidate, or distract your young player. Most of the time, your own back yard will work, but if your dog is magnetized by the great outdoors, start inside.

Hold the end of the lunge line in one hand and the puppy in the other. If your pup is too large to be carried, or is already an adult, either hold the dog back by the collar or harness or find an assistant to help. Do not let your dog go until he is actively

Hold your puppy or restrain him by his collar or harness while the toy skitters. You want to build excitement.

Let puppy go when he is desperate to get to the toy.

Work hard to keep the toy about six inches away!

struggling to get to the toy. Place your young player on the ground and immediately move the toy away – ideally, he will immediately lunge for the toy while you keep it moving about six inches in front of his nose. That six inch distance is quite important for a dog who is actively chasing. At that distance, your dog can practically taste the toy and you'll have your hands full just keeping it out of his mouth! Strive to maintain that distance.

Remember that you should be erratically flipping and skittering it through your area. The stronger the puppy's forward motion, the faster and more erratic you can be with the toy – squirrel panic!

If your pup is hesitant, let the toy rest on the ground occasionally, like a bold squirrel who knows he can escape. When moving the toy, keep it a little further from the puppy - maybe several feet or even more! Your goal is not to let the puppy grab hold of the toy; that comes later. If he does grab it while you're trying to keep it away, that's okay because it means your puppy really wanted it! Overall though, at this stage, your goal is to get the puppy to believe his forward motion causes the toy to escape in a panic.

Brito almost had it; the toy is panicking!

Continue playing in this fashion for one or two minutes, but no more. Quit if your dog becomes bored or starts to leave, and next time have a much shorter session. Darting and chasing at top speed is exhausting; don't play until your puppy flops over!

If your young player shows avoidance-type behaviors — refusing to look at the toy, walking away with nowhere to go, and so on — you may have been too aggressive or intimidating with the toy, or he may already have preconceived negative ideas about toys. Move the toy in a less erratic fashion and at a greater distance until he is confident and moving towards the toy again. Or, find a helper to restrain the puppy while you play gleefully by yourself. If necessary, go back to the stage where he's watching from a window or a crate.

This dog is beginning to show avoidance of the toy. STOP!

It is absolutely normal for some puppies or dogs to ignore the toy. They are not in avoidance, they are simply not interested. Don't give up! Denise's young dog Brito could not have cared less about that crazy piece of rabbit fur on the end of a lunge line when he was first exposed to it. He wanted to explore the world instead! And then one day, he suddenly went insane trying to get that toy. From there his interest was not linear; some days he was crazy intense while other days he wasn't very interested at all, and still others he vacillated between these two extremes within one session. However, over time his prey drive became stronger, to the point that even in a very exciting public place he wanted to play.

Here Denise is bringing the toy in much closer to her body.

Repeat this sequence several times a day until your puppy is madly dashing around the yard after the toy and trying to grab hold of whatever piece is closest. Your total daily play time should not exceed five or ten minutes.

Once your puppy reaches this stage, start to shorten the whip portion by wrapping it around the handle until the toy is fairly close to your body. Continue to move the toy in an erratic fashion. When the puppy chases the toy with great enthusiasm on a short lunge line close to your feet, it's time to let the puppy get hold of the toy. Your dog's behavior will determine the rate of forward progress, so this step could occur in the first session or after several weeks.

Catching the Squirrel

It's time for your dog to catch the squirrel – if he can! Your job will be to make it possible for him to get it, but only if he puts forth great effort. The victory is much sweeter if he believes he has earned it, so don't make the game too easy. If you attempt to move the toy to the puppy because you want him to win, not only does that diminish how much he wants it, but the movement of the toy towards him may also frighten him out of a prey mindset. Remember, squirrels are not suicidal. You must quell your desire to get the toy in the dog's mouth!

This squirrel made a mistake. Brito caught it!

Keep the toy active even after the dog catches it!

Move the toy in an erratic fashion — left, right, quick jumps up, but keep it mostly down on the ground. When your dog is putting out maximum effort, make a mistake. You can either change directions across the dog's path or flip the toy up like a leaping squirrel just as your dog is approaching it. Most puppies will be able to grab some part of the toy.

Your next move is critical: do not give up. You are a squirrel who is in danger of losing his life! Panic! Try to escape. Squeak. Face away from your dog and maintain gentle yet constant pressure, movement, gentle jerks, and tension on your line. When your dog loses his grip or becomes unsure – and he will, all pups make a mistake eventually - you MUST take this opportunity to escape.

Now run for your life! Skitter on the floor for several seconds and then snap the toy up to a safe place and out of reach of your puppy. Make sure you talk to the puppy in a cheerful voice at this time. Talk about how much fun you had and how you can't wait to play the game again. Do not play again for the rest of the day – squirrels rarely give predators an immediate second chance. Let him sleep on what happened instead.

The squirrel escaped!
Do not let your dog catch it too quickly at this point.

After the first day, it's okay to continue playing after the toy has escaped, but never engage in so many repetitions that it becomes boring. If you struggle with playing for too long, setting a timer might be helpful to remind you not to push so hard. Repeat this lesson until your dog goes crazy at the sight of the toy on a line.

At this point, your dog will likely hold on to the squirrel once he catches it. He may even lie down and possess it. If he does, just wait, tell him he's very clever, and then watch for an opportunity to escape! However, if your dog starts to chew on the toy, become active again to discourage this habit. While chewing or consuming prey is a normal part of the prey sequence, it's not useful for our purposes so we normally try and cut it off before this point is reached.

An insecure or unsure dog may grab the toy, but never quite commit to it. Instead, he will follow the toy with it in his mouth but without clamping down on it. While it's great that he is trying to stay with the toy, you want to encourage stronger jaw pressure on it, so keep the toy moving away from him with an occasional slight upwards or sideways pull. If possible, vibrate the toy in the dog's mouth for a few seconds before it escapes. Let him think he almost got it!

Once your dog is consistently grabbing the toy and staying engaged with it, move in closer when you play, but don't be in a great hurry to get your hands on the toy. While

Brito is learning to be comfortable close to Denise's body.

some dogs can move quickly from a toy on a lunge line to playing directly with you, others will take weeks to be comfortable with your presence up close. This is not a race; take your time and build a strong foundation of love for the game.

Denise has worked her way up to hands on the toy.

Once he's comfortable with you being close, drop the lunge line on the ground or hold it without any tension and see if you can pet your dog, gently push him, or pat his sides. The goal is to add small amounts of pressure - just the amount that your dog can accept it and remain strong! If your dog remains engaged or gets more excited, that's great. However, if he drops the toy and walks away, you added too much pressure.

Denise adds pressure in small increments and over time.

Back up and make yourself less threatening. Again, there is no hurry; take your time!

By this point, your pup should be tenacious and grabbing hold of the toy tightly. At the same time, you should have moved to holding the toy itself. Congrats! You've been roped into a game of tug! Go ahead and play tug with the lunge line still attached to the toy. Just remember that if the toy ever falls out of the dog's mouth, the toy must try to escape! Grab the handle of the lunge line and restart the game.

Let Him Win!

When your dog is holding on to the toy with tenacity and for longer stretches of time, you can drop the lunge whip and let him win! Cheer the whole time, approach and pet your dog – but do not touch the toy early on in the process. He won it so you must not steal it. After a short period of time, maybe thirty seconds, go back to the end of the lunge line and wait for the puppy to either start chewing on the toy or to put it on the ground, and then snap it out of his mouth and restart the game.

Brito won!
Denise celebrates with him by clapping and petting him, but she doesn't touch the toy right away.

If your puppy starts well but does not remain engaged, go back to videotaping your sessions. There is nothing as effective as a video camera to help you see where you might be causing accidental pressure. What is your reaction when the puppy lets go? Do you stop the toy's movement, even for a second? Do you stop being playful and happy? Do you try to move the toy back towards the dog's mouth? Do you physically move into the dog's space? Are you maintaining gentle but constant tension and motion?

Tighten Up the Game

Now that you have a very playful puppy who is comfortable when you hold the handle on his toy and move into his physical space with varying degrees of pressure, it's time to remove the lunge line. When you do, it's best to play in the same place that you worked with the lunge whip initially.

Remove the whip from your drive-building toy and keep the toy high out of the puppy's reach until you are ready to begin. You will want your dog to come to the game with

Now Denise and Brito start the whole process again - without the lunge line.

Brito grabs the toy easily now. It's much harder to keep the toy away from the dog once the toy has been removed from the lunge line.

a high energy level, so you may want to have your pup watch you play alone or with another dog before involving him. Once he's feeling lively, have him join you. Kneel down on the floor with the toy in your dominant hand, behind your back and out of the puppy's sight. If you find it difficult to kneel on the floor, you can sit on a chair or stool. Pull your pup in close to you; if he's small, you can hold him on your lap with one hand. If he's larger, either hold him back by keeping your arm around his neck and chest or hold on to a wide buckle collar or harness.

As soon as the puppy is secured, flip the toy out as far as possible in front of you and move it erratically. Your goal is to be the squirrel again, using the same moves as you did with the lunge whip. Move the toy quickly away from your dog, then in an erratic zigzag pattern back and forth in front of you. One of the easiest patterns is a figure eight with lots of extra flips and zips! Occasionally have the toy disappear briefly behind your back, only to quickly re-emerge into view. The toy should be moving in a wide arc out as far away from your body as possible, and never close enough for your still-restrained dog to reach.

Your puppy will show some kind of physical reaction to the toy. If the reaction appears to be avoidance, either by trying to get further away or by carefully avoiding looking at the toy, go back to using the lunge whip, but slowly shorten the lunge line until you can hold the toy in your hand and your puppy shows curiosity and interest in pursuing the toy. Then try the above steps again. There is no rush; some dogs need time to get used to this new game.

Start play on the ground.

Stand up when the dog is very comfortable.

Add pressure by hovering, adding body contact, and so on.

If your puppy's reaction is to struggle to get free of your grip to get the toy, let him go! Keep the toy about six inches in front of his nose until your dog is so determined to get it that it's impossible for you to keep it away from him. When he does grab the toy, it is critically important to put the right amount of pressure and motion on the toy. Too little pressure and the puppy will either try to lie down and chew the toy, or he will develop the habit of munching and shifting his grip up towards your hands to create action. He might even get bored by the toy's lack of response and disengage from the game. On the other hand, if you use too much pressure or rip the toy out of his mouth, the puppy will give up and stop trying to play. With young pups, it takes time for their jaws to develop to the point that they can apply enough pressure to play hard, so use a give and take movement with the toy. You want him to always feel like he's on the verge of either victory or defeat; only his behavior determines the outcome.

Nancy is facing away from Kiyo as they play; this is an excellent way to build confidence.

The right amount of pressure will also allow you to constantly feel your dog's mouth as you move the toy. Most of the time, the motion of the toy should be relatively continuous and side to side in direction, but every once in a while, go ahead and panic. This occasional jerk will both keep the puppy awake and prevent lazy bites or letting the toy hang loosely in the mouth. If the dog lets go of the toy, you must again make the toy become a squirrel determined to escape. Make sure your dog is fully engaged again before allowing him to have another chance.

The easiest motion is to make a figure eight with the toy. This allows it to constantly change direction, keeps it in front of you, and helps keep it fairly far away from you, especially when passing the toy in front, so that your dog doesn't worry about being too close to your body. To avoid receiving an accidental bite, keep the back of your wrist towards the dog (like twirling a baton) with the dog on the outside of your arm when going to your sides. With this motion, the dog's entire body will move once he grabs the toy. The result should be less work for you and more work for him!

Note the figure eight motion that Denise is using. She leans as far forward as possible to move the toy out and away from her body. This helps reduce pressure on the dog so he can concentrate on the games.

Let your dog win on the occasions he is most tenacious. Always pet and praise the puppy for a minute or so after he wins before restarting the game. If the puppy is still holding on to the toy, you'll be starting from an existing game of tug rather than from a prey reaction. If your puppy's primary interest is to take the toy away to chew, you do not have to release the toy. Tugging is about the interaction between you both.

Ending the Game

Eventually you'll want to end the game and take the toy back for good. This is simple with a small or medium-sized puppy: to get the toy back, simply pick up your puppy. Most puppies drop the toy within a few seconds if you pick them up. As the toy falls from his mouth, tell him he's a good boy and walk away while holding him. Leave the toy on the floor and come back for it later.

Pick up a small dog or puppy to get your toy back.

A larger dog can be "cradled" to get the toy back.

If your dog is too large to pick up, lift his front end off the floor by cradling him underneath his chest and then wait him out. Do not touch or try to remove the toy from his mouth. Instead, tell him he's wonderful so he doesn't think that you are attempting to correct him. Eventually, he will drop it. When he does, leave it on the floor, distract your pup, and take him out of the room. It's fine to lead him by a wide collar or harness out of the room.

The reason we do it this way (take the dog away from the toy and return for it later) is so that your dog does not think you've stolen his toy. If he does, it will be harder to get him to release it the next time. If you want to go back to playing after he's dropped the toy, just keep him restrained and then pick the toy up and start the toy motion again.

You can play as often as you like, but always quit with the dog wanting more. Keep in mind that most dogs won't work with intensity for more than a couple of minutes at this stage.

Verbal Encouragement

Dogs vary in their need or desire for verbal encouragement. Some do better if you stay quiet during the initial drive building phase so they can concentrate on the game of chase, grab, tug, and kill. If you find that your puppy looks at you rather than at the toy, stop talking. Look at the toy yourself, completely absorbed in what you are doing. When the puppy is holding on to the toy, you may encourage him quietly, but stop if it appears to become a distraction. And don't growl at your puppy! Most dogs view that as a threat and the next thing you know your puppy won't want to play anymore. On the other hand, if your dog seems concerned about your silence, go ahead and encourage him verbally while maintaining your focus on the toy.

Building Confidence in Your Pup

You should begin to see signs of growing confidence in your pup. He may get very excited at just the sight of the toy. You'll notice improved physical coordination and determination to get the toy. He will start to fight harder to keep the toy in his mouth, tugging and shaking it, and trying to get as much of it in his mouth as possible. He will be willing to get closer to your body.

Kissing Edge while playing tug adds pressure!

Nancy places more physical pressure on Kiyo.
Kiyo handles it fine!

When this happens, it's time to slowly increase the physical pressure you place on your puppy. Begin to occasionally touch the puppy with your free hand as you keep the toy moving with your other hand. Don't let the toy stop moving; we don't want him to let go! Gently pat your pup on the sides, using a firmer touch as he gains confidence and builds trust in you – but never hurt or frighten your puppy, nor allow anyone else to do so. Work the toy closer to your body, or even higher up on your legs. Try playing tug while you're standing up rather than kneeling on the floor.

Any signs of insecurity — growling, shifting grip, letting go — means you need to go back to easier play and add pressure in smaller increments. For example, if the puppy lets go when you pull him up onto your lap with the toy, try pulling him towards you but not onto your body.

Your goal is to keep your dog engaged and in prey drive despite an increase in pressure. This will help "toughen" your dog so that he learns to channel minor stress or distraction into play rather than letting go and concentrating on the external stimuli. With time, this skill will become extremely valuable. Dogs who can focus on interaction with you by playing tug at a dog show or in other challenging or novel environments have a HUGE long-term advantage over dogs who cannot.

Growling During Play

Although there are some dogs who are very noisy players, watch your dog's overall behavior very carefully if he starts to growl during play. Predators do not growl when they kill prey unless they feel threatened. If he growls and then releases the toy, growling is likely an early warning sign that your dog is not feeling confident and you need to scale back the amount of pressure you are applying. If, on the other hand, your dog is a verbally expressive dog who growls due to enjoyment, then it's probably okay, but you'll want to make sure he doesn't get over-aroused. As a general rule, try to keep the dog slightly under the point where the growling begins.

Zoey practices her game of tug at the dog show using her leash as the toy!

Taking it on the Road

All good training goes through the three step process of teaching, proofing, and generalization - and that includes the game of tug! We have covered the first two steps by training the behavior with interactive play and proofing it by increasing the physical pressure. Now it's time for generalization.

When your puppy plays with confidence in a familiar environment, it's time to leave your familiar training spot. As always, when starting generalization, start small! First work in your front yard, then in the driveway, then on the sidewalk, then in the neighbor's yard, and then down the street. Always ask for much less from your dog in new environments; don't be afraid to go all the way back to the toy on a lunge whip if that is what your dog needs to be confident. With time, your puppy will learn to play with you in a wide range of environments and around many different distractions. The more places you play with your puppy, the more confidence you'll have to work with when it is time for your first performance events.

When you find that your puppy is highly motivated to play, goes for the toy as soon as an opportunity presents itself, and bites down hard enough to play a strong game of tug, it's time to introduce a new toy. The more variety you work with, the more options you will have for toys later on.

Conclusion

Some puppies will work through the entire sequence from the first exposure to a toy on a lunge line to playing strongly with you in a new environment in just a matter of days. Others will take weeks or even months. There is no set amount of time for this process. Take it slow, enjoy the process, and never be afraid to go back to an earlier step if you run into trouble.

Once you've worked your dog through the steps outlined in this chapter, you will have a usable game! Your dog wants to play, engages with you in a wide range of environments under varying degrees of distraction, and increases in energy as a result of your toy interaction.

Congratulations! You have trained a tugger!

Chapter Seven
Switching to Training Toys

Most dogs would be glad to stay with drive-building toys forever because they're really fun! The dog gets to perpetually chase a pretend squirrel while also getting the opportunity to play fight while biting a toy. For the trainer, however, there are several reasons to move the dog from a drive-building toy to a training toy. This chapter will cover why and how to make the switch.

This toy is perfect for a young bearded collie but will not be appropriate when she's full grown.

With a large or powerful dog, training toys are not optional! A shorter, stiffer toy allows a small handler with good technique to play effectively.

Why Switch?

One of the biggest reasons to switch to a training toy is that drive-building toys are hard to control. Once your dog gets a strong hold, the whippy action that makes them so appealing also makes it very difficult to control where the dog's body goes. Indeed, a strong dog can easily whip the owner around in circles, which is NOT much fun for the trainer and often leads to the trainer choosing not play anymore.

Drive-building toys also make it very difficult to create a clean release without conflict (we will discuss this in depth in an upcoming chapter). To get a release, the squirrel must die. When the squirrel gives up fighting, predators naturally put the prey down on the ground so they can consume it. Unfortunately, long whippy toys are quite difficult to hold still so that they can appear dead. Even if you do manage to hold the toy still long enough to get the release, many dogs will simply grab under your hands for another piece. It's a frustrating problem and is discouraging for the trainer.

Chasing a frisbee is fun because of the prey action of the toy,
whereas biting the ball is fun for the biting action itself!

Of course, switching to a training toy means that you will lose prey action, so your dog must learn to play for bite satisfaction instead. Unlike prey action, where the dog chases a toy skittering on the floor, bite satisfaction is the actual interactive fight with the prey – or in this case, with you. To make it interesting, the bite surface must continue to move and be somewhat prey-like, although you will skip the prey action step. Most dogs take to this reasonably well as long as you've put in the time to build a good foundation with the toy. Age is a factor here. Many dogs seem to lack the maturity to take a toy for interaction alone until they are adults.

If you have no trouble managing your dog using a soft whippy toy, and your dog gives it up when requested, then you may not need to switch at all. But if you find the idea of using a short, stiff toy either appealing or necessary then read on!

Making the Switch

At the end of the last chapter, your puppy was starting the process of generalizing toys of varying sizes, types, and textures. That training is going to pay off now.

Go back to your lunge whip and tie a training toy on to the end - preferably a rather soft one. Start at the very beginning and get your dog leaping and chasing the toy.

*Lyra is back to the lunge whip - this time with a
training toy attached.*

When he is well engaged, allow him to grab the toy. If he gets the rope instead, try grabbing the toy yourself and presenting it horizontally in the air while encouraging him in an excited, enthusiastic tone of voice. You could also try moving it erratically on the ground while encouraging him. You will notice that it is harder to make your training toy erratic, but your dog's prior training with drive-building toys should have developed a strong enough desire to bite to overcome this.

When your dog is comfortable with the new, stiffer toy on the lunge line, remove the training toy from the line and return to sitting on the floor. It's easiest if you use a

*Denise now creates prey action with a training toy
before releasing Lyra to catch it.*

Acre's mom adds pressure by touching his flank.

toy with one handle, keeping that handle tucked into your hand as you move the toy across the floor in an erratic motion. When your dog engages with the toy, play a rousing game of tug!

Over subsequent sessions, repeat the sequence you followed with the drive-building toy: slowly stand up, play harder, and add pressure in the form of body contact, minor distractions, and new locations. Once you are working at this stage with a training toy, you will no longer need to engage your dog using prey action; your dog will play for the interactive fight alone.

The last step is to stand up straight, show the dog the toy, step backwards, and encourage him to jump up and bite a toy being held horizontally in front of you. Do not hold the toy by the handle - that is not a stable target! You want it to be reasonably steady so the dog can get a good hold. Be careful not to move the toy towards the dog, allowing him to come to the toy instead.

This is the correct presentation of the tug toy.

Presenting a toy hanging vertically is likely to end with bitten fingers.

Getting a Deep Bite

When your doggy predator grabs the toy, it is likely that his initial bites will be with his front teeth because he's grabbing whatever he can get. There's nothing wrong with this, but most dogs are happier if they can move the toy to the back of their mouths so they can get a very strong grip with their molars. This desire is particularly strong with the working breeds. We call this process of moving the toy from the front of the mouth to the back of the mouth a re-bite. Many (but not all) dogs are more comfortable

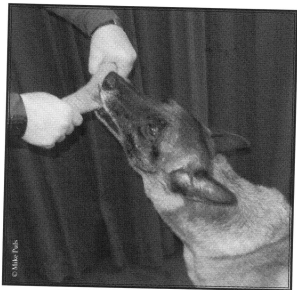

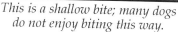
This is a shallow bite; many dogs do not enjoy biting this way.

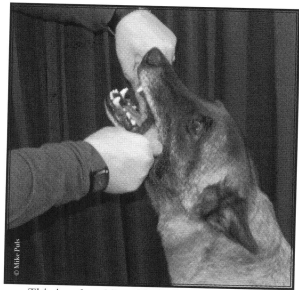
This is a deep bite with the back of the mouth.

and satisfied when biting in the back because they recognize that the odds of winning the game are much higher with a more secure hold. When prey is in the front of their mouths, it might escape! So give your dog a chance to bite deeper into the toy.

To encourage a re-bite, make sure your dog's head is level or facing slightly down, and then hold the toy still for just a brief second. Many dogs will take that opportunity to quickly push in and grab the toy in the back of the mouth. If this does not happen within one second, go back to playing and try again in five seconds or so. If your dog does take a deep re-bite, reward that with a great game of tug!

If you notice over time that your dog does not choose to take a deeper bite, and if it does not affect your dog's ability to release the toy when you'd like it back, then don't worry about it. Play in whatever manner your team is most comfortable.

Comfort and Safety

Now that your dog tugs well, you'll need to start thinking about how you intend to play this game so that both of you remain safe and engaged.

Let's start with the dog. Dogs frequently move their heads from side to side, but it is very rare to see them nod in an up and down fashion. A dog's neck simply was not meant to move this way so do not pound your dog's front feet into the ground while you whip his head up and down. Keep your dog safe! Instead, move the dog from side to side in figure eights. If you're struggling to do this (it can be harder if you have a strong player), study the photos in the remainder of this chapter to develop a style of play that is safe and appropriate for both the dog and the trainer. You can drag the dog behind you with feet on or off the ground or you can pull him next to you. Pick something that works for both of you!

Handler comfort and safety is also important. As a general rule of thumb, you will be happiest if you keep your body straight with your shoulders aligned over your feet and your hands and arms close to the body. Think "elbows in".

*Denise demonstrates good posture; her back is
straight and her arms are close to her body.*

*Denise's arms are too far from her body and she is
bent over. This is very likely to lead to handler injury,
especially if the dog jerks in any direction.*

We also discourage the dog from pulling backwards on the toy and fishtailing from side to side because doing so causes the trainer to be pulled off balance. The trainer often ends up moving in circles because she is trying to stay on her feet. This is fun for the dog but miserable for the trainer. There seems to be a very strong genetic component to how dogs choose to play tug, and while it can be modified, it's not normally worth the trouble. Instead, try the following ideas:

With your dog next to your side, bring his front feet off the ground and wrap your free hand around the dog's neck. Keep the dog in very close to your body and pull the toy out and away from the dog.

Raika's front feet are off the ground and Denise's arm is around her neck, while her other hand pulls the toy forward.

Another way to reduce handler discomfort is to play tug by holding the toy with one hand and pulling the dog behind you with the dog's head against your body. Many dogs will wrap their legs around your leg when you do this, taking even more pressure off the handler.

Cisu is pulled behind Denise with Cisu's head close to Denise's body.

Bring the dog in as close to your body as possible and between your legs.

Cisu is between Denise's legs and straight down - this gives Denise maximum leverage and control, leading to a comfortable play session.

Another method for saving the trainer's body is to put the dog between your legs from behind, and pull straight up on the toy. The dog will pull down, and your legs prevent the dog from fishtailing.

Raika is between Denise's legs; a very easy and comfortable position for the handler.

Finally, it's important to note that fishtailing is often associated with dogs who are too highly aroused. They growl, munch the toy, thrash their heads, and weave their rear ends from side to side. In order to stay on their feet, their trainers rotate in a circle, constantly facing the front of their dogs and often walking in the dog's direction to try and keep their balance. This actually adds pressure to the dog, which makes the behaviors worse. When this pattern starts, the trainer no longer wants to engage the dog in tug because it is simply too much work. If this describes your situation, take a good look at your dog's level of arousal. Is it time to scale back to a less intense style of play?

Conclusion

Spend some time finding the best style of tug for you and your dog. An experienced trainer can play with a very large dog and still remain safe and comfortable, but there do need to be some rules to make it work. Work hard to find a method of play that allows both of you to enjoy the game. The remainder of this chapter includes additional photos to help you find a play style that works for you and your dog using a training toy!

Denise has two hands on the toy and walks while she pulls Raika. This is a comfortable approach for Denise.

*"Absorb" the impact of a fast dog by allowing the
dog's speed to turn the handler's body.*

Drop your weight by bending your knees and keep your hands in close if you are working with a very strong dog.

Here Denise plays tug with Cisu's dumbbell. The hardness of the object gives Denise maximum control.

Denise is holding Raika's ruff with one hand and pulling up on the toy with the other. This gives the handler more control.

Denise is holding on to the two handles of a toy, which allows Cisu to "thrash" her head. This is very uncomfortable for the handler!

Cisu has her feet up, which is hard on the handler.
Discourage this by pulling the dog in between your
legs as much as possible.

Note the low presentation in front of Denise's body
causes the dog to jam herself.

This is a much safer presentation for a stronger dog
because Denise can absorb the impact
of Cisu's launch.

*Erica shows good posture when playing tug with a drive-building toy.
Note her straight back!*

The goal in training is to avoid conflict (competing impulses) as much as possible, but for many dogs, releasing the toy creates a good deal of conflict. A dog must be taught to drop the toy when asked – after all, play is all well and good, but at some point we want to get some work done too! This chapter will teach you how to get a release while minimizing conflict. We do this by helping the dog understand that letting go of a toy doesn't mean the fun is over.

The Two Toy Game

We start teaching the release through the Two Toy game. This is actually a fetch game because the dog learns to let go of one toy so he can chase another. This lowers the strong need for continued possession of a single toy since he knows there will be another available on release.

When introducing this game, it helps to have two very similar fetch-type toys, such as balls on a rope. Start by showing your dog one of the toys. When he is interested in and excited about it, toss the toy about six feet away. As soon as your dog grabs the first toy, call his name and show him the second one. If necessary, use an excited voice and erratic toy movements to gain his interest. When he's interested in the new toy,

Duzi practices the two toy game...with three toys!

Napi is about to chase the second toy César is holding.

toss it about six feet in the opposite direction. Ideally, he will race towards the second toy, dropping the first toy somewhere along the way. Then you can pick up the first toy and activate that one. Make it look enticing and exciting, then toss it back in the first direction. You will repeat this process, throwing the toys back and forth about six feet in each direction with you in the middle. As your dog races back and forth from one toy to the other, he will drop the toy he is holding to get the next one.

The next step is to hold the first toy in your hand until your dog drops the one he is holding - only throwing the toy in your hand when your dog releases the one in his mouth.

Courtenay and Reiker are playing the two toy game with a ball.
Note that Courtenay holds the first toy until Reiker releases the one he's holding.

Reiker holds one ball and looks at the other in Courtenay's hand.

Reiker releases the ball he is holding.

Courtenay immediately throws the ball she is holding.

Courtenay picks up the first ball.

And the game starts all over again!

The Two Toy game encourages a sequence of grabbing, then dropping, then grabbing again. This helps your dog understand that releasing a toy isn't the end of a game, but rather a way to make the game continue.

The Toy Switch Game

The Toy Switch game is similar to the Two Toy game because it teaches your dog that letting go of a toy does not end the game. The difference is that the Toy Switch game is not a fetch game, but an interactive one. In this game, you will not throw the second toy; you will hold it in your hand and make it exciting to create the release of the first toy.

For this game, it's best to work off leash, but if your dog must be on leash, use a long line and step on the leash so both of your hands are free. Choose two toys that have the same level of value for your dog (using identical toys tends to ensure that, but is not required). Put one toy either in a pocket or within easy reach.

Note the second toy in the handler's pocket.

Time to switch!

Now, begin a vigorous game of tug. Once your dog is fully engaged with the first toy, bring out the second one and stop actively engaging the one that your dog is biting. If your dog tends to run off with the first toy, keep a hold on it, otherwise drop it altogether. The toy your dog is holding is now dead - it's in his mouth, but it isn't doing anything interesting – while the second one is now the total focus of your movement and excitement. Slap it against your leg or the floor, verbally encourage your dog to "get it," and move it quickly and erratically. Your dog will likely drop the first toy in order to get this new, exciting toy. Great! While playing another vigorous game of tug with this new toy, put the dead one behind your back. Then switch again.

Your dog will learn that as soon as you stop creating motion and tension with a toy, he should drop it because you will have a new, active toy for the game. Possessing a passive toy isn't much fun compared to the exciting second toy! Again, this helps your dog learn that letting go isn't the end of the game at all, just part of the process. Both of these games are easier to teach to young dogs without much tug experience, although older dogs can learn them too. Take the time needed to teach them because mastery of these games will make a formal release much easier.

Chewie holds one toy but now it is dead. Jo then makes the other toy active to entice Chewie to switch.

The Release

Teaching a formal release will require your dog to learn that sometimes letting go of one toy does not cause another one to appear. Instead, it causes that first toy to come back to life instead!

To accomplish this, play with a short, stiff toy that can be held tightly in your hands. While your dog is holding it with a deep bite in the back of his mouth, kill the toy by locking up your body and refusing to move – not even an inch. Of course, this is easier with a small puppy, but even an adult dog in full play will have a hard time if you bend your knees, straighten your back, and keep your elbows and arms close to your sides. When you do this, it is important that your dog's head is level with his body; if his muzzle is pointing up, ensure that there is no tension. If you pull up, it will inadvertently create more fight.

With both hands on the toy, bring your hands in close to your dog's muzzle and wait. Almost all dogs will release (or begin to release) within fifteen seconds if you

When you ask for the release, don't move!

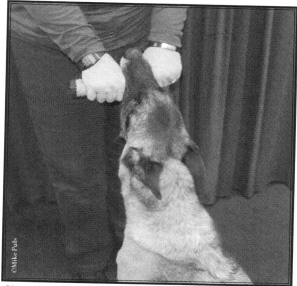

Keep your hands close to the dog's muzzle on the toy. Do not move.

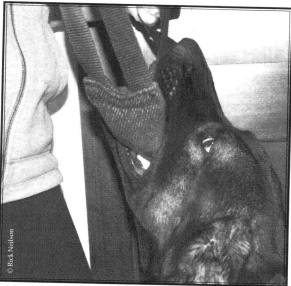

Note that this handler is holding the handles rather than the toy; this makes it impossible to lock up and it is likely that this dog will not release.

handle the toy in this fashion. As soon as your dog's mouth is off the toy, move your fingers over the bite surface for only one second to help your dog understand that he shouldn't try to take it back. This step is not required for all dogs and can usually be eliminated after a few days.

Over time, your dog will begin to release almost immediately. When you notice that your dog begins to release as soon as he feels your body lock up, add your verbal release cue. Then reward the dog's cooperation by immediately playing again! This part is extremely important so we will repeat it with capital letters:

Even with a large dog, the technique for creating a release is the same. Lock up your arms, bend your knees, straighten your back and DO NOT MOVE.

REWARD YOUR DOG'S COOPERATION BY IMMEDIATELY PLAYING AGAIN.

Lyra is almost off the toy so...   *...she gets an immediate re-bite!*

Immediately means just that - not five seconds later, and not after you snap the toy up and away from the dog's reach. As soon as his mouth is off the toy, quietly tell your dog he is good as you cover the bite surface with your hand, and then quickly move your hands out of the way, snap the toy out, and tell him to get it! Do this every single time until your dog is completely clear on the relationship between 1) your body stiffening and the toy going dead, 2) opening his mouth and moving it off the toy, and 3) your instantaneous and enthusiastic re-start of the game.

The reason this method works so well is that over time your dog can predict that the lock up/release cycle will lead to another fabulous game, leading him to release sooner and sooner. Even better, the dog actually looks forward to it, because the best game in the session always comes after the release! Now you have a clean release with no conflict; you and your dog are on the same team and are interacting cooperatively!

Take the time to develop a strong response to your release cue before using toys as a reward in training. Most puppies or young dogs can master this cycle extremely quickly, usually within days if they have never experienced any form of fight in the release portion of the game. Dogs who have learned pressure techniques to get them to release (pulling up on collar, opening their mouths, raising your voice, etc.) will take much longer to master this because pressure techniques create conflict – resistance and refusal to release in stronger dogs, and demoralize softer dogs, leading to a poor attitude towards play. Go to great lengths to avoid this scenario because retraining a cooperative release is much more difficult than getting it right in the first place.

If you choose not to switch your dog to training toys and prefer to stay with a drive-building toy, the process for teaching the release is the same. Simply ensure that there are no extra pieces of the toy hanging down for your dog to grab after the release. Hold the toy as steady and taut as possible between your hands, and....wait.

Teaching the Highly-Driven Dog

Unfortunately, we cannot end this chapter here because some people have a very different type of dog. These dogs were born playing and always have a toy in their mouths. They take the game very seriously. Their trainers often cannot believe that the above method, which might work with a softer or less driven dog, is going to work with their dog.

It works.

Play tug with a short toy to ensure a deep bite before asking for an out.

Lock up.

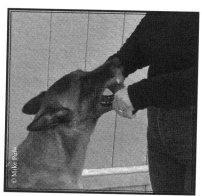

Wait for a release.

One second off the toy.

Explode in to re-bite!

The key to a clean release – consistently and without struggle – is to refuse to fight over it. Never. Not even once. This is doable if you follow the rules. Once again, they are:

1. Start the game with a short, stiff training toy.
2. Allow a re-bite to ensure a deep bite.
3. Play tug with your dog.
4. Place two hands on the toy, close to your dog's mouth on both sides. Make sure the handle is in your hand and not dangling.
5. Bring your arms in against your body.
6. DO NOT MOVE!
7. Reward the release with another game of tug. No "misses"!

There are a few differences between training the release on a more moderate dog and on a highly-driven pup. For the high-drive pup you will not need to do the drive-building work with the lunge line; your dog doesn't need his drive built up! Instead, your games will be much calmer because genetics will take care of the desire to play. You will also introduce the release simultaneously with play.

You must avoid using force or pressure to create the release. Not only will your pup grow to become so strong that physical force becomes quite difficult, but you will also find yourself needing more and more force. As a result, your dog will learn to fight with you, not the toy, and you will become highly frustrated. This additional fight simply excites these types of dogs, encouraging them to hold on even harder. In other words, you have created conflict, and quite a bit of it at that.

To regain control with your dog, you must remove the conflict. To de-escalate this situation you need to become quieter, not louder. This means you need to:

•Quiet your voice. Lower your tone. Speak softly and clearly. Do not yell or threaten.

•Quiet your emotions. You must become calm and controlled. Dogs can very easily sense stress and frustration, and those emotions can amp up an already anxious or tense dog, which will only make the situation worse.

•Quiet your body. Eliminate unnecessary movement. You may need to apply more frontal pressure to your dog – the exact opposite of what we do when we are trying to build up a dog's confidence. Face your dog squarely when requesting the toy, but without leaning over or becoming threatening. Remember, you are calm.

•Quiet your hands. When your hands are on the toy, lock them up against your body and do not move them. You will not move EVEN AFTER THE DOG RELEASES. This is critical. Your dog should move back away from the toy rather than you moving the toy out of the dog's mouth. You can then move your hands over the bite surface to prevent him from grabbing the toy again, but you will not move the toy one inch.

If your dog has experienced years of handler conflict, you may be in for a long wait. All we can say is get comfortable! If you really, truly do not move, your dog will let go eventually. Once he does, wait two seconds and immediately re-engage your dog with the toy. Now you can become friendly, exciting, and lively. You are a team player! Convince your dog that pleasing you is in his best interest, both in terms of your emotional interactions and the quality of the game being played. If you want to let your dog win the toy on occasion, that's fine, just keep him on a leash or cradle him so he can't go anywhere. Your dog can hold the toy for as long as he wants. This could be several minutes. When he does drop it, leave the toy on the ground and move the dog away from the toy.

This handler holds her dog's collar and waits until he chooses to drop the toy on his own.

If you are not strong enough to wait your dog out, you will need someone to help you train your dog until the clean release is in place. Sometimes it helps to back the dog into a corner to reduce the possibility of fishtailing. You might also want to do this when your dog is already a little physically tired (but not mentally - mental strength is required to process the new information and training).

There can be no training of behaviors for a toy reward as you go through this re-training program. You can work on behaviors for food or other motivators, but your toy training will be strictly that; toy training.

The Really, Really Difficult Release

You've tried everything. Your dog stands in front of you with clear eyes, a quietly wagging tail, a calm disposition... and a toy lodged firmly in his mouth. He is not avoiding you and there are no signs that he is in conflict. Rather, it seems that this is a dog with a very high level of possessiveness and no great desire to change that. Holding the toy is an eight out of ten. Playing tug is an eight out of ten. And since a bird in the hand is worth two in the bush, well, your dog sees no point in releasing the toy.

If you find yourself in this situation, we have one final approach, but you will need to pre-train two behaviors before you start.

First, teach your dog a solid default down behavior that will override everything else. Work on this obsessively. Any time you ask for a down, he should drop like a stone and stay down while you move around. Work until this behavior is reliable with or without the possibility of a reward.

Train the down cue to the point where your dog always drops and stays down, even under great distraction.

Simultaneously, work on teaching your dog to switch toys as described earlier in this chapter. Working with your dog on a leash, play a very mild game of tug. After a short period of time, release the toy, get a second toy out, and make it as exciting and appealing as you can. The goal is to incite your dog to drop the first toy; when he does, immediately allow him to have the second toy and play a rousing game of tug the way he likes best. Repeat this process until seeing a toy emerge causes your dog to drop the one in his mouth to go for the new one.

Now we're going to combine these two behaviors. Engage your dog in an extremely mild game of tug with the hardest and stiffest toy you can find. Have a second (identical) toy in your back pocket that the dog doesn't know about. Play on a leash so you can prevent your dog from leaving if he does not respond quickly and easily to your down command. Now, let the toy go, wait a few seconds, and ask your dog to lie down. Cue your release, which should have been mastered in the Two Toy game. Most dogs will cooperate out of habit. He may also immediately drop the toy since holding a toy and lying down is not gratifying for many dogs.

Ryker lies down on cue and drops the toy but keeps his head over it.

If your dog drops the toy, immediately present the second toy high over his head and simultaneously release your dog from his down. Play a good game of tug, then slow down the game until your dog is calmer. Pick up the second toy quietly, then let go of the one you are holding. Step on the leash if your dog tries to leave. Repeat the process of cuing a down and following with a toy above his head several times. Your dog should soon begin to drop the first toy as soon as you request a down because he's anticipating the second toy.

Ryker goes for the one high above his head.

Pick up the second toy quietly.

Repeat the process.
Note that Ryker is now more relaxed.

Begin reaching for the toy, but then stop and use the
toy in your hand instead.

When this is going well, after you ask your dog to lie down, make the tiniest motion toward the toy on the floor before pulling out the second toy and playing. When we say tiny, we mean just that: either quickly glance at the toy on the floor, or bend your body slightly towards it. If your dog remains focused on you, take out your second toy and play hard while ignoring the toy on the floor. Continue with this technique, making progress one tiny step at a time, until you can actually touch the toy on the floor. The key to success with this method is keeping the dog's focus on you, not the toy on the ground. Most dogs can succeed if they watch you, but if they look down at the toy, they become overwhelmed and grab it again.

If your dog failed to release the toy on the down cue, go ahead and show the dog the second toy from your pocket. You can smack it on your hands, create a mild prey reaction with that toy, and walk around a bit yourself, always returning to your dog and offering a chance to play. Present the second toy above the dog's head so that if he does drop his current toy, he won't be distracted by the first toy landing between his feet.

If your dog fails to release on the down cue, show the second toy from behind your back.

If you must, walk away from your dog and ignore him for a minute, although he must hold his down stay while you do this. If he cannot hold his down, then you need to go back and put more time into this step. As you walk around, look at the toy in your hands and wave it around, making it appealing. Then return to your dog and try again. He can choose to either lie on the floor holding a dead toy, or release it and have a wonderful game with you.

If your dog grabs the toy off the floor in response to your movement towards the dog or the toy, simply give him another cue to lie down. Do not pay any attention to the toy in the dog's mouth. That toy is invisible as long as your dog is holding it.

Eventually, your dog will be able to win a toy in tug play, down with it in his mouth, release it to the ground, and look up at you expectantly. You will be able to reach down and touch the toy on the ground without causing conflict and then play with your dog using a second toy. Once you've mastered this, you will be able to pick up that first toy from the ground and play with it.

Hopefully you've realized that during the time you are retraining the release, you should not train with a toy. Use food instead.

Denise had to go through the really, really difficult release training with her dog Cisu when Cisu was slightly over a year of age. Cisu had many excellent skills for her future in IPO and obedience, but her lack of release was a serious problem. Denise could feel her frustration mounting as Cisu grew stronger and Denise could no longer get objects back without an enormous struggle. Denise knew something needed to change when she realized she no longer looked forward to training sessions.

To fix this, Denise stopped training with toys and the team went back to food rewards. They had separate training sessions every day to develop a clean release off tug toys, balls, and ring objects like dumbbells and gloves. It was about a month from the time that Cisu could down on command without a release to the point that Cisu could down and release in one step without conflict. It was several more months before Denise no longer had to ask for the down to get the toy back. In the end, Denise had a very powerful dog for many dog sports - and no conflict.

In contrast, several of Cisu's close relatives continued to struggle with this issue because they would not let go of anything once it was in their mouths. This included dumbbells for obedience and protection helpers for the sport of IPO, effectively eliminating them from competition altogether. Until the day that Cisu passed away, she would occasionally forget how to release a toy. A quick reminder with the down release cue would help her remember, and the session could continue without a struggle. It may take time and effort, but creating and maintaining a clean release is well worth your while.

Adding in Work

There is one last step that needs to be described for the release - especially for those highly driven and difficult dogs. When your dog can release the toy, wait quietly while you pick it up, and then re-engage in a game of tug, it's time to add work back into the equation.

As always, we encourage you to start small. Give one small cue - like a sit - and then an instant release to play. Follow this with three or four repetitions of releasing the toy and immediate play. Then do a release, a simple cue, and more play. Over time, you will be able to obtain more behaviors before the dog earns the toy. You will also be able to reduce the amount of release-to-play sessions your dog needs to stay in a cooperative frame of mind.

Ryker has been cued to sit, which is quickly followed up by a throw of his toy.

Conclusion

This training works, but it takes time, persistence, and the ability to move at the dog's pace. Remember, many highly possessive dogs have been bred by us to be possessive. Now we have to take responsibility for training the types of dogs that we have created - and to do so with kindness and respect.

Chapter Nine
Problem Solving for Tug

This dog's expression suggests avoidance.
Take the pressure off!

It is difficult, if not impossible, to predict all of the possible problems a team may encounter on their way to learning how to play tug effectively. However, there are some problems that are quite common. In this chapter, we will offer some ideas to help overcome those typical challenges.

Dog is not Interested and Avoidant

Hands down, the biggest reason dogs do not play tug is the behavior of the trainer. Sometimes trainers want their dogs to play so desperately that they aggress towards their dogs: approaching rapidly, shoving the toy in the dog's face, and expressing disapproval when the dog does not respond as desired.

If your dog shows avoidance behavior when he sees you with a toy – sniffing, turning away, yawning, lip licking, and so on - do some serious soul searching. Lack of interest in toys is relatively normal in an untrained dog. Outright avoidance is not normal – it was created somewhere by someone.

You must take the pressure to play off the dog. Put all of the toys away for a period of time before starting over with the lunge line, and then go very, very slowly. When you create a problem in training, it will likely take twice as long to get to your goal – one round to fix the damage and a second round to make forward progress.

This dog is not interested but is not avoidant either.

Dog is not Interested, but not Avoidant

If your dog simply stares at the toy on the lunge line but makes no forward motion towards it, even after multiple exposures in a low stimulation environment, there are a few things you can try.

One method that often works is to tie a plastic bag to the end of the lunge whip. The crackling sound will get some dogs excited and moving forward. If the bag piques your dog's interest, don't let him catch it! Instead, stuff some paper towels into the bag and resume play. Now if your dog manages to get to the plastic bag, let him rip it up and shred the paper towels.

If that doesn't work, test the dog's willingness to play in a different location. This will help you make sure there is nothing seriously distracting or intimidating in your usual environment that you're not aware of.

You can also have another person try playing with your dog. Sometimes dogs have rules with their trainers that don't exist for other people. For example, if a trainer has never allowed her dog to play in a physical fashion and then asks the dog to be wild and crazy, it's common to see confusion and an unwillingness to play.

The same holds true with dogs who have experienced a good deal of compulsion in training. These dogs often become rather passive when interacting with their owners because they are waiting to be told what the correct behavior looks like. Since playing tug is anything but a passive activity, these dogs struggle with their owners but thrive when a new person enters the game. This happens because there are no preconceived notions about right or wrong behavior with this person. If the dog shows interest with the new person, it is likely that the original trainer can take over again.

A final option is to tie a plastic bag to the whip and add food. As a general rule we do not like to add food to toy play since we believe it puts the dog in the wrong frame of mind, but when all else fails, why not?

Dog Lacks Sustained Interest in Public

A lack of sustained interest often happens when the trainer has expectations that are too high. Dogs initially play in very small bursts. When Denise first started working with her young terrier, he could not play in public for more than three seconds at a time. It was months before he could lock in on a mutual game when there were distractions. This is normal.

It is normal for a young dog (or a young human!) to struggle to pay attention when distractions exist in the environment.

Figure out what is typical for your dog, then reduce your expectations by 90%. This allows you to end the game on a positive note rather than having the dog walk away or mentally disengage. Slowly increase your expectations as your dog shows an ability to maintain focus.

Meanwhile, when playing at home, double check your technique using a video camera. Once your dog gets started, you must work hard to keep that toy no more than 6" from his mouth - any further and the dog may not feel that he can catch it. Ideally your dog will be so close that he can almost taste that squirrel if he just puts out a tiny bit more effort! That degree of focus and intensity will help your dog learn to shut out all possible alternatives in public.

Dog Won't Bite the Toy

It is common to see dogs who love to chase the toy on a line, but balk at actually putting the toy in their mouths. If this describes your dog, then our first question is,

"Are you sure you have a problem?" Denise has had several students with dogs who love to chase the toy, but have no desire to catch it. Chasing a rabbit in prey mode is a very strong drive for them, but catching and fighting simply isn't a natural part of their personalities. If they ever got close to live prey, it is likely that they would simply let it go rather than seriously attempt to catch or kill it.

Remember, to use a toy as a motivator, you need the dog to behave in a MOTIVATED fashion when the game is over. If your dog is aroused, focused, and willing to work for that degree of a reward, you do not have a problem. For some dogs, the interesting part of toy play is chasing the toy, not grabbing hold and play fighting. Admittedly, it is easier to train and trial a dog who accepts bite satisfaction over prey play. On the other hand, you cannot force a dog into biting hard on a tug toy if that behavior is uncomfortable for him. You can still use your drive-building toys during training sessions and get quite a bit of benefit. Simply wait until you wish to reward your dog, drop the toy down on a line, and let your dog chase the toy for 10 or 15 seconds. Snap it up (as if it escaped!) and call the dog back to work.

This puppy is having a wonderful time chasing; she doesn't need to bite the toy to enjoy the game. Note the handler's non-threatening posture.

You must never forget that the purpose of a motivator is to maintain energy and fun for your sport. Don't get hung up on your preconceived notions about what a dog MUST do. Your job is not to please someone else or to meet your instructor's interests. Your job is to learn to play, train, and motivate the dog in front of you. Sometimes this will look different than you had originally expected.

Dog has a Poor Grip on the Toy

This is often related to the previous problem. The dog doesn't really feel comfortable biting the toy, while the trainer tries to keep it in the dog's mouth. Rather than focusing on making the dog hold the toy, think strictly in terms of engagement. Is the dog still visually tracking the toy even after he lets it go? If so, go back to using the toy for drive-building and have fun.

If you think the dog is disengaging because he finds an alternative more interesting (for example, the dog's eye is caught by something else in the environment), then each time the dog lets go, snap the toy up and go right back to asking for work instead of play. If your dog is indeed enjoying the toy at a level which motivates him, he will begin to stay engaged longer when he realizes that the cost of letting go is the end of the game.

Keep in mind, however, that lack of engagement might be your dog's way of telling you that he is strong in prey interest, not in fighting with the toy. You can honor that interest by allowing him to chase without any real expectation of grabbing hold. Sometimes when the handler relaxes, the dog's responses get stronger due to a lack of pressure. In a few weeks he may be grabbing the toy with real intent.

Uh oh. She let go and lost her prize!

Dog is in Pain

Another common reason dogs won't stay engaged in tug play is physical discomfort. Dogs have no way of telling us when they don't feel well. While sharp pain will normally elicit a yelp, many dogs endure chronic pain with very little indication.

If you ever notice a change in your dog's normal behavior, particularly if he played well before but will no longer engage, it's important to consider the possibility of a physical problem. The possible sources of pain are numerous: cracked teeth, normal teething, chiropractic issues, joint problems, growth issues, and soft tissue injuries are just a few of the problems that may be the culprit.

Is Bella tired, bored or in pain? It can be hard to tell!

If you have ANY reason to suspect physical pain, give your dog the benefit of the doubt. Don't force your dog to do something that he is telling you he does not want to do. Sometimes it's best to take a break for a week or two and see if things improve on their own. If they don't, then you need to consult a healthcare professional. Keep in mind, however, that pain is often invisible - even to a professional. You may want to talk to your veterinarian about a trial period of pain medication. If that suddenly makes an enormous difference in your dog's behavior, you have the answer, even if you're still not sure of the cause: your dog is experiencing pain.

Dog Won't Return the Toy to the Handler

This is a common problem with dogs who are more interested in owning dead toys than in fighting to kill them. There are a couple of things you can do to raise a dog's interest in play fighting while simultaneously lowering his possessiveness. If your dog is growling, snarling, or snapping when you move close to the toy, or if you feel uneasy or threatened, you need to stop toy play immediately and consult a qualified behaviorist. If your problem is mild, however, we have some suggestions.

Review the Two Toy Game. Denise has one toy and Quiz has the other.

Start by reviewing the Two Toy game with tugs. Your dog should learn that giving up one toy causes another one (that happens to be in your hand) to become very active. This process of letting one go and returning to you for the other does wonders for creating a team player.

Then, make a point of pulling your dog AWAY from your body when you play tug. This will only work with a small to medium breed of dog or with a puppy of a larger breed, so try to get the return to handler habit cemented early. When the dog wins, opposition reflex will bring him back into your space rather than away. It's you and the dog against the toy!

If your dog is beyond that age or phase of play, then try this: working in a small space, let the dog win the toy extremely easily. The goal is to make the dog feel that the fight was so minimal that it was basically non-existent, like a 50 pound dog catching a mouse rather than a squirrel. When there is no real fight, most dogs will appear confused; they were ready to give the fight their best shot, but then the contest ended before it really began.

After the dog is allowed to have the toy with almost no effort, back away from the dog.

Denise is pulling Brito away from her body to encourage a better return.

Get down on the ground and turn away so that the dog is looking at your side. Start talking cheerfully to your knees while watching your dog in your peripheral vision. A high percentage of dogs find this completely non-threatening and come close. Praise your dog - but do not touch the toy.

Work on this until your dog will sit very close to you. You can start this process in the house with one of the dog's toys (not a training toy) so there is no issue with getting it back when you are done. You want to lower the dog's possessiveness while getting him to enjoy your close proximity. Make sure there are no other dogs around when you play this way, or the dog will likely feel worried about the other dog stealing the toy, creating conflict.

If you can get to the point where the dog will sit with you while he is holding a toy, the next step is to try petting the dog. When that becomes comfortable for him, get up and move away. You want him to follow you. Next, stand up, but keep your upper body oriented away from your dog. Again, your goal is to get him moving into your space. Do not look at the toy while you move through this process, just interact with your dog. Now you can try gently pushing your dog away from you.

Quiz is possessive! He has collected all of his toys.

See if the opposition reflex causes him to come back to you even more quickly! When he becomes comfortable with this game go ahead and touch the toy (don't pull it!) and then quickly move away from the dog before he can move away from you. Continue gently pushing the dog or tapping the toy and moving away. Take your time getting to the point of asking for the toy back.

You'll be amazed at how quickly this builds up a dog's interest in play fighting, but it works because your dog learns that he will always win the toy. While this process takes place, do your formal training for food so that you don't have battles that undo all of your good work. Eventually, many dogs will literally follow you around and push the toy into your hands to get you to engage. Now you can go back to using the toy as usual. This entire process might take minutes, days, or weeks - be patient!

If your dog would rather shred the toy and eat it, select your toys carefully. These dogs do better with harder toys made of leather or jute and with no filling inside. The lack of filling helps to discourage the shredding behaviors while the hard exterior feels more like a stick for retrieving than a rabbit for eating.

Dog Won't Play When the Toy is in the Trainer's Hands

Some dogs are fine with the toy when it's on a rope, but once the trainer holds the toy, they no longer find it interesting. These dogs are often sensitive to the fact that it is

no longer a small toy with a few ounces of weight; it is now attached to a human being who is well over 100 pounds.

In this case, check both the amount of personal pressure you're using as well as your technique. To reduce your personal pressure, orient your body so that the dog is more sideways to you, and allow the dog to swing behind you during play. This reduces pressure on the dog, and allows him to feel stronger while you work on his core confidence. In addition, make sure that the toy does not go dead once you have it in your hands. Work hard on your technique to duplicate the action the toy creates when it is on the long line.

Pulling your dog behind you by a tug toy builds confidence!

Not a tugger? Try tugging with a ball or throwing the tug!

Dog Plays Ball but not Tug

If your dog is an avid retriever but doesn't show the same enthusiasm for playing tug, get a toy that is designed for both. These toys are designed to be thrown first and then used for tug when your dog returns them. Examples include balls attached to a rope (Gripper balls, balls on a strap, Kongs on a rope), and Frisbees (which can be made of nylon, jute, or rubber). You can also play fetch with a tug toy in order to increase your dog's enthusiasm for it when you add the game of tug back in. We recommend you avoid toys with tennis balls because they tend to encourage gnawing and wear down your dog's teeth over time. Likewise, with Frisbee-type toys, soft nylon or jute material is fine, but most hard plastic disks aren't appropriate for games of tug.

It is very normal for a dog to have a preference for either a ball or a tug toy.   Games with a ball involve running and prey behavior, and less of the intense predatory drive of a dog chasing a tug toy on a line. Games of fetch don't normally involve a fight - it is a simple retrieve and return so the whole process can be repeated. Both games are wonderful depending on your interests at a given moment, so if your dog is strong in playing ball, put more time into building your game of tug - and vice versa.

Dog is Easily Intimidated by the Trainer

Practice playing with your dog on your side or pulling your dog behind you (don't forget to keep moving – you should still seem like a squirrel who is fleeing). You might also want to try getting down on the ground and playing at the dog's level. Avoid eye contact until the dog is more comfortable, and do not growl at your dog! Many dogs take this as a threat and will let go and walk away.

Videotape, videotape, videotape! If you were a three-year-old child, would you be comfortable playing with an adult expressing your behaviors, postures, and mannerisms? Are you relaxed and smiling, or do you look like tug is serious business? Work on softening your demeanor and remember that this is supposed to be fun! It helps to think in terms of the number system of energy. If your dog is giving a 3, then you want to give a 4. If you give a 10 instead, you are going to intimidate your dog and cause him to avoid you. This is a much bigger problem than not playing with the toy at all.

This handler's posture is not threatening. She is on the ground and has her side to the dog.

Dog Munches on the Toy

This problem is normally caused by lack of tension on the toy. A dog cannot munch on a toy that has constant light tension because if he does, the toy will be pulled out of his mouth. Any time your dog opens his mouth, he has just given the squirrel a chance to escape. A dog engaged in the game will not loosen his grip on the toy.

The exception is a dog who is simply trying to readjust a front-mouth bite to a deeper bite. In this case, the rebite normally happens when there is a minor break in the game with a lack of tension, but the dog will clamp down firmly as soon as you regain tension. If you do not want your dog to rebite, then do not allow the toy to stop moving - but be aware that a front-mouth bite is frustrating for some dogs. If you have an interest in the protection sports like IPO or ringsport, you must learn to allow and even encourage the rebite, although that topic is beyond the scope of this book.

Dog Bites the Handler's Hands

We have seen so many dogs held responsible for their trainer's poor tug play technique that we no longer recognize biting hands as a canine problem. Tug play is a mechanical skill which must be mastered, so while people may get their fingers bitten for a variety of reasons, they are almost always TRAINER induced errors.

One common error is presenting a toy vertically in the air while holding it on only one end. This makes it close to impossible for the dog to bite the toy, especially if the toy is swinging in the air. Dogs tend to target the most obvious part of the object. If your arm, hand, or fingers are the largest horizontal possibility, you risk being accidentally

Play with drive building toys on the ground, not in the air.

Training toys must be presented horizontally to offer an obvious target.

bitten as the dog attempts to get a good hold on the toy. Be very careful to present the toy in a manner that allows the dog to target properly. Because a dog's muzzle is horizontal to the ground, the toy must also be presented horizontally. If you are using a drive building toy, keep it on the ground so your dog can trap it between his muzzle and the ground. If you are using a training toy, present it horizontally in the air.

Another common reason handlers get bitten is failure to maintain constant motion and tension on the toy. When the toy goes dead, the dog will come forward to try and get more of the toy in his mouth, which inevitably includes your fingers. Tension on the toy makes your dog concentrate on holding rather than on shifting his grip.

A final reason trainers get bitten is failure to hold the toy still after the release. Once the toy is dead and you have asked for it back, everything must stop. The toy must stop and the dog's mouth must stop. The dog should look up at you in expectation of either another bite or more work with you! If the dog continues to move, stand still and simply cover the total bite surface with your hands and fingers until he orients to you. Denise has done this hundreds of times and has never been bitten by anyone's dog in the process. Resist the urge to pull the toy away from the dog once he lets go. Dogs often perceive this as stealing, which not only complicates the release, but also makes it more likely that the dog will try to grab it back from you. The dog should move away from the toy; the toy should not move away from the dog.

If you consistently use the correct training toys, good target presentation, constant tension and motion while playing, and if you have trained a clean release, 99% of bites to your hands will simply disappear.

Dog Shreds the Toy

A dog cannot shred a toy that is in motion, so do not let the toy stop moving. If the dog starts shredding it after he's won the toy from you, focus on getting a fast return. You can run away from the dog, lower your posture so you are more approachable, and practice behaviors that raise the dog's interest in fighting with you over the possession aspect of the prey sequence. Also, consider toys without stuffing – they aren't nearly as much fun to eviscerate as toys that are stuffed.

Dog Disengages Immediately After Releasing the Toy

Disengagement is normally an avoidance behavior caused by too much pressure. When you see avoidance, go back to playing simply for the joy of the interaction. Train with food while you rebuild your personal toy interactions with your dog. Spend time together with toys, and make a point of working in relatively dull environments where there is very little to do that is more interesting.

We also see this behavior in dogs who are stressed by the environment, and whose trainer is trying to use the toy to overcome the dog's concerns. The end result is a dog who plays desperately, but as soon as the toy is gone, the dog goes back to checking out the environment for danger. Attempting to override a dog's safety concerns is not healthy because it teaches a dog to work in a frantic state rather than in a driven one. Do not start playing with your dog until he has given you clear signals that he is ready and able to engage with focus.

Conclusion

While this chapter cannot possibly cover all of the challenges a dog and handler team might face, we hope that the combination of detailed instruction in the earlier chapters with the addition of this problem solving chapter will help you on your way to the most positive, enjoyable, and engaging tug play possible!

Chapter Ten
The High Drive Dog

High drive puppies want to bite!

Some of you have probably read the preceding chapters with absolute puzzlement. From the time your puppy arrived home, his teeth were attached to everything from your skin to the couch. Your dog has never seen an object that he didn't want to bite and kill. Your clothing is shredded from all of the attacks launched by your killer baby (often from behind and as high as shoulder level). You are covered in pinprick holes from those sharp puppy teeth and have bruises up and down your arms.

You've tried redirection to a toy, but your puppy does not want the toy - he wants your clothing and your flesh. The more you squeaked "ouch!" (as your trainer directed), the more your piranha took that as a cue that he was winning - and went in for the kill. You've even tried correcting him by picking him off the floor by his scruff to show him you mean it - and he turns into a 10-pound, snapping, snarling Cujo, oblivious to your attempts to subdue him. Indeed, the harder you fight to gain control, the worse the situation gets. At this point, you're seriously wondering if buying this puppy was the biggest mistake of your life.

High-drive dogs of certain breeds are very challenging puppies, and the challenge does NOT lie in building their drive. It lies in their nature; their genetic temperament. You've got a Ferrari but you're used to station wagons.

Your main goal should be simply surviving the first six months when your puppy acts more like a wild animal than a precious little baby. During this time, you should be learning to intelligently balance drive and control. You need to develop the ability to clearly recognize overarousal versus usable drive. At the same time, you must learn that simply calming your dog down is not the answer; that approach simply creates intense frustration. If you have a pressure cooker dog, you must create a release valve. Keeping the lid on and pretending like everything is calm inside is not the answer because the pressure is building up whether you choose to see it or not. And at some point, there will be an explosion.

Basic Survival Strategies

High-drive dogs often need a LOT more physical and mental stimulation than other breeds of dogs. Give your pup as much time to run and play in a safe place as possible. You'll be much better off if your puppy can wear himself out chasing a jolly ball.

If someone tells you that you need to withhold all toys so that your puppy will want to play when you do, take another look at your dog. Do you really think this is a dog who will turn down an opportunity to play with you when you want to play?

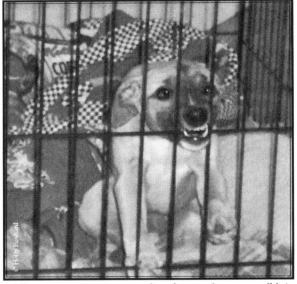

A truly high-drive dog does not need you to nurture and encourage his tendencies to play. He needs you to channel them. Go for survival; give your dog as many challenging toys as you can find. Food toys, puzzles, large balls, chewies, stuffed kongs, and whatever else you can find or dream up. Do not feed meals out of a dish; use them for training or serve them in a puzzle toy.

Allow your puppy as much safe exercise as possible!

High-drive dogs will often offer quite a bit of focus for work early on, so take advantage of that to imprint a variety of foundation behaviors in your puppy. These dogs are like sponges who will soak up all the training you can manage. When your puppy comes out of the crate in the morning, raring to go and excited simply to be alive -

this is your prime training time! After a good night's sleep, most puppies show maximum drive with their greatest frustration tolerance. As a high-drive puppy gets physically and mentally tired, he tends to lose his inhibitions. He becomes a cranky toddler who really needs a nap, but doesn't want to sleep. This is when he's more likely to react without thinking and use his teeth liberally.

Forget personal play without a toy in your puppy's mouth - it won't go well. Arousal and biting are very closely linked in high-drive, biting breeds, so accept that it will probably be quite some time before he can play with you without engaging his teeth.

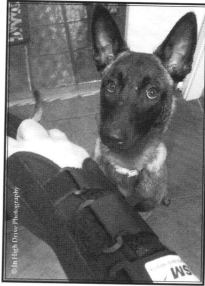

Forget personal play with a high drive puppy; the timing isn't right!

Socialization

Work hard on socialization; intense biting breeds are often TOO handler focused. They want what you have so badly that they never look around, never truly experience the world, and therefore, never learn that it is a safe place. Make a point of taking your pup places so he can learn about the world. Do not bring out a toy to distract him or redirect his behavior; use food if he gets too intense. Remember, the goal is for him to satisfy his curiosity about the environment.

A thirty-minute socialization outing will wear out your puppy more than you might expect, both physically and mentally. When you return home, put him in a crate even if he does not seem tired. Just because he's moving around a lot does not mean that your pup can forgo a nap. It is very normal for tired puppies (and children) to move MORE than normal because they are fighting their need to rest. After a period of exercise or mental stimulation, put your puppy to bed in his crate with nothing to do but sleep - no toys or activities to keep him occupied and awake.

The Relationship between High Drive, Arousal, Fear and Aggression

Speaking of socialization and arousal, you may have been advised to redirect your puppy to a toy if he becomes nervous or frightened in public; to play intensely to get his mind off of whatever is bothering him. Let's consider this strategy for a moment.

If your dog is distracted by (but not afraid of) something and you redirect to a toy, then you are pairing a neutral stimulus with a toy. Over time, the presence of neutral stimulus should redirect the dog's focus back to you, giving you a lot of energy to work with. There is no real danger to this approach, except that you might end up with a dog who struggles to relax in public. Since he has only channeled his arousal into active play, he's never learned how to move into a calmer and more relaxed state. While inconvenient, this may not be a real issue for many handlers.

If your dog has a very mild fear of something and you redirect him to the toy, it's counter-conditioning: pairing something that evokes a very mild fear with an enjoyable game. With time, the dog begins to associate the mildly fearful stimulus with a fun game. Again, while this does nothing to teach a dog to be calm in novel places, it does help teach your dog to focus on you, not the environment.

Now, let's consider a dog who is so worried or fearful that you are aware of the problem. What happens if you redirect a worried dog from the source of his fear (possibly other dogs, people, or maybe something like a stick on the ground) on to a toy? While you might classically condition a positive response to those stimuli, it's also quite possible that your dog will attach his feelings of fear and anxiety on to the toy. Playing with the toy is now associated with unpleasant emotions.

If your puppy shows a mild fear of noise, allowing him to play with a bag of cans is a great way to desensitize him.

Classical conditioning can go either way depending on what is strongest in the situation. You may have heard that classical conditioning depends on the order in which things are presented; bell rings, food appears, and soon the bell predicts the food, which causes the dog to drool in response to the bell alone. And this is true - in the lab.

Out in the real world, though, it's much harder to control all the variables. With more moderate or typical dogs, fear outranks almost everything in intensity. As a result, fear is highly likely to trump play. This is often called going over threshold.

With highly-driven dogs who have been genetically designed to interact no matter what, it can be much trickier to tell if they've gone over threshold. It is quite possible that you will actually poison the activity, food, or play with the overwhelming fear from the stimulus. This happens because the dogs are hard-wired to find certain objects or activities so strongly self-reinforcing that they will engage with them no matter what. It's often more than an enjoyable activity; it becomes an obsession.

But it gets worse. This becomes a huge problem because you end up with arousal from the activity combined with the negative emotion of fear. While it is true that some high-drive dogs will always play, it is not necessarily true that they are enjoying the activity or receiving stress relief from your games.

In many breeds, fear, aggression, and biting a toy while over threshold (that state where the dog is not able to think rationally or clearly due to either stress or excitement) are linked. You risk creating a dangerous dog if the external stimuli becomes too overwhelming while the dog is playing with you. Arousal from the activity combined with the negative emotion of fear results in a powder keg just waiting to explode, and your dog can easily drop the toy and redirect that fear and aggression on to whatever - or whoever - is nearby.

If your dog will never need to live as a normal pet, walk in public spaces, attend crowded dog shows, or interact with a variety of people under a variety of circumstances, then this approach to socialization might work just fine. But if your goal is competition, your dog will need reasonable levels of sociability with novel dogs, people, and environments, and we'd strongly recommend against encouraging your dog to channel fear and/or aggression into toy play. Socialize your dog properly and allow him the opportunity to develop normal and confident responses to the world.

Katydid plans to socialize herself as she escapes her kennel!

Appropriate Toy Training

Be prepared to give your high-drive puppy a good deal more training, exposure, and play time than other dogs. Not because he needs it for his future as a performance dog, but because he needs it to stay mentally occupied. Many of these dogs would happily work for twelve hours a day. Excessive crating for management purposes often happens because their owners are too busy for them, but this is truly cruel. If you do not allow your puppy appropriate outlets for both his physical and mental energy, it could lead to neurotic behaviors such as excessive destruction and self mutilation. Imagine locking a genius child in a closet because you don't have time for him. MAKE time - or get a different type of dog!

All of your toy training should be focused on toy-related skills. Do NOT use a toy to reinforce other behaviors that the puppy might know. Instead, focus your toy training time on a combination of building play technique and control. If your interest is performance, and if biting technique is not important to you, then work with whatever tendencies your puppy is showing you. Trying to calm him down by refusing to engage will simply frustrate your puppy because he's not getting what he needs. If your puppy truly needs to fight with you to have a great time, then you'll have to fight. And your puppy will need to learn the rules. Right now!

Playing tug with objects is not an aggressive activity. It's for fun!

Let's take a minute to define what we mean by the term "fight." When we say fight, we're not talking about aggressive behavior at all. We're talking about the degree to which your dog has to give his all to win a game. Some dogs need to believe that they have used up every bit of effort and energy to truly enjoy the game; they want to win, but they also need to feel that they earned that victory! With these dogs, winning is only satisfying if they feel that losing is a possibility.

Think of it as the canine equivalent of the human game of tug-o-war. To be an entertaining game, there needs to be a sense of a real contest; winning too easily is boring. Imagine if you were playing with a five-year-old. You know that you can win easily, so your mind is occupied with what you're going to have for dinner while you are playing with the child. But what if you were a very competitive adult who really wanted the physical release of a serious game of tug-o-war? Then you'd be miserable playing with a five-year-old. Frustrated! Irritable!

If you need that release, then what you want is a well-matched partner who is just one notch less capable than you are. And so it goes for high-drive dogs. If your dog requires a serious fight to be satisfied, then give him one! How long you fight depends on the puppy. Some do best for just a few seconds while others do best for a long time - maybe even a minute. Just remember that when it's time to ask for the release, there must be no conflict or collar pressure.

Teach your puppy to switch between toys (both tugs and balls) easily. Spend a lot of time teaching and practicing the Two Toy and Toy Switch games we discussed in Chapter 8. Not only are you teaching valuable skills of toy release and cooperation, you're also giving your puppy some much needed exercise while interacting in a

Using a lunge line and a toy can help your puppy get some much needed exercise.

mutually enjoyable manner. Soon, you'll find that your puppy will release the first toy, even if it is still moving, when you cue that a second alternative is available. This is very useful for high arousal sports and training!

If you wait too long to develop this skill, it will become harder and harder to switch the dog from a possessive frame of mind to a prey based one. You are making the release easier by teaching this skill early on. You're also teaching your dog to let go quickly, even in a high drive state. Dogs who can do this will eventually be able to work for a toy reward, and when the time comes to go back to work, the dog can be sent directly to the next behavior with no formal release at all - just biting to working and back again in a seamless manner.

End a Toy Play Session with Food

Playing to the point of exhaustion is rarely a good idea because puppies from high-drive lines actually become MORE committed to holding on to the toy when they're tired. They lose their capacity to think clearly and to make good decisions. Find the amount of play or training time that keeps your puppy engaged with you without going over the top with frantic behavior. That might be one minute or five minutes; experiment with how many repetitions of any game or exercise is best for your puppy.

When you think your puppy is getting tired, switch from toy play to food play. This switch will help your puppy gear down to a lower level of arousal so that he can relax at the end of a training session. If necessary, get your puppy to switch to food by putting the food directly into his mouth or in front of his nose. Make sure you use very smelly, highly desirable food for this. If that still does not create a release, hold the toy steady with one hand and start throwing food on the ground in front of you. You want the puppy to redirect from the toy to the piece of food as if it were prey. Once the puppy lets go of the toy in favor of the food, quickly hide the toy and play food games for several minutes.

Using food will get your high-drive pup back into a clearer state of mind, moving him from the high arousal state that toys create to the calmer state created by food. Ideally, we want the puppy to completely forget about the toy for a short period of time. Using food in a rapid fire manner will cause that to happen. Keep up a high rate of food delivery (try for 20 tiny pieces in the first minute) to prevent frustration. That rate of reinforcement can be reduced to whatever level makes sense for your pup as soon as you can see that he's calmed down enough to think solely about the food.

When your puppy is looking at you with bright eyes and a wagging tail over his sudden food festival, it's time to work on some skills using food as the reinforcer. At this point, your puppy still has energy, but he can now concentrate on working with you. At the end of your skill building training, you may (or may not) want to repeat the sequence all over again, beginning with the toy play and working back to skill training with food.

Switch to food play before your puppy becomes over aroused by the toy.

Teach Calm Behaviors, but Don't Try to Make Him Calm

High-drive puppies should also work on basic calming behaviors like impulse control and mat work, but that does not mean that you should substitute calming behaviors for appropriate energy outlets!

Here's a human example: imagine that you are a teacher with a very bright and high energy child in your class - twice the energy of every other child. You need to work on teaching that child that he can sit calmly at his desk for very short periods of time. When he has done that, you will allow him to release that energy by encouraging him to move his body and use his mind in appropriate activities. In addition, you will provide lots of one-on-one time for pleasant interaction and relationship building activities with you - his teacher - so he learns that you control access to really interesting information or activities. Those periods of being calm must alternate with periods of excitement or you have the "pressure cooker without a release" problem; an explosion

Teach calm behaviors, but remember that won't make him calm!

of frustration and energy is bound to occur.

If you put all of your energy into calming a child who is truly boiling over with mental and physical energy, you are not changing the temperament of the child by forcing him to be still. You are showing disrespect for his true nature and trying to make him something he is not. This creates a situation where he dreads your presence because you are not relating to him on a level that he finds engaging. The likely result of this is avoidance - of you. The same is true with high-drive dogs with trainers who do not attempt to engage them at a level that they find satisfying and enjoyable.

If you take a minute to think about it, the best way to engage another person (or dog!) is to start where he is and then see if you can engage him in your interests. If you are working with a very high-energy puppy who wants to bite more than anything else, that's fine! Start with that - play lots of games of tug in a manner that is satisfying for him. Over time, you can include more and more calming behaviors, adding to your expectations slowly and with care. If you attempt to assert your interests all at once (Stop biting! Sit on your mat for 10 minutes! Don't pull on the leash!) your puppy will not enjoy your company. This will have enormous ramifications for your long term relationship.

Appreciate the dog you have. Your puppy is bred to move, to bite, to think, and to engage, not to sit passively while the world moves around him. Respect that. At the same time work on small periods of self-control activities - but only when he is fresh and most able to think, not when he is exhausted and overwhelmed at the end of the day.

Conclusion

If you start where your puppy is and understand what he is bred to do and how that works for you, then you can raise your high-drive dog to be a tremendously powerful competitor. But you must develop your relationship so that you are on the same team. Do not allow conflict to develop, because he actually thrives on fighting. Allow him to express his drives and energy while also helping him develop his ability to be calm and thoughtful. Make sure he sees the world with proper exposure and socialization. Teach an early release off the toy. Do not play to the point that he is over threshold and out of his mind; if you do, you are creating a conditioned emotional response of over-excitement towards you, work, and play. Set yourself up for success; strive for a balance between excitement and calm from your first days together. And be patient. It gets better.

Chapter Eleven
Fetch: The Basics

So far, we have spent a lot of time discussing the game of tug, but tug is just one type of play that can be useful in training. Another wonderful option is the game of fetch. Fetch is really a retrieving game: the owner throws an object, the dog chases it, brings it back, and the game begins again. Fetch can have very little personal interaction between trainer and dog, but when combined with tug, it can become a very engaging game indeed!

Why We Play Fetch

While a typical pet owner usually plays fetch with her dog as way to exercise him, dog sport trainers play fetch for several additional reasons.

First, fetch is an excellent reward for a dog who is at a distance. We believe strongly in rewarding the dog for position, so we always aim to deliver the reward as close as possible (in both time and space) to the place where the dog performed the behavior. It is much easier and quicker to fling a fetch toy to a dog who is forty or fifty feet away than it is to try rush a food reward out to the dog.

Trainers also play fetch because it creates instant energy. While it takes little to no effort

Games of fetch are excellent for exercise!

Fetch is an easy way to increase your dog's fitness level for competition dog sports.

for a dog to accept a cookie from your hand, most dogs will take off after a thrown toy at a dead run. Of course, to a large extent, the dog's speed and response are a function of the dog's interest in the game. If your dog has no interest in fetching objects that you have thrown, there is no value in using fetch as a reinforcer. Fortunately, many dogs easily take to the game with relatively little encouragement on the owner's part.

Fetch is a great way to build up a dog's physical stamina, especially for the quick and intense physical efforts required in many dog activities. Running back and forth on a field during a game of fetch is an enjoyable and effective way to build both sprinting ability and endurance.

Another benefit of fetch is that it can free up a dog who is stressed or mentally overwhelmed by some aspect of work. Alternating a toss of a fetch toy with a difficult training concept can keep the dog's head clear. Unlike tug, which brings out a desire to fight, games of fetch are more prey oriented. That leads to a clear mind as expressed by bright eyes, forward ears, and a relaxed (yet alert) posture. While some dogs lock up into a stalk mode when playing tug – almost freezing into non-motion – games of fetch rarely have that effect.

Games of fetch can also build the dog's working relationship with the trainer. Fetching objects is a powerful motivator for many dogs, and it builds great value into the one who controls the ball – you! If a dog is willing to work hard at what you want (dog sports) in exchange for what he wants (a game of fetch), you are well on your way to creating a high-energy working companion.

Finally, many of us play fetch simply because it is fun! We love to watch our dogs sprint away at full speed, then return quickly with tongues lolling out the sides of their mouth, eyes bright and open with expectation. Most of us choose to own dogs because we like dogs; watching a dog light up at the possibility of a game of fetch is highly motivating for many owners.

A great reason to play fetch is to have fun!

Teaching a Dog to Fetch

Much like the game of tug, teaching fetch is a mechanical skill. Fortunately, most people find that it is less complicated than playing tug, and dogs seem to have fewer negative reactions if the trainer plays poorly. While it is common to see a trainer accidentally create avoidance to the game of tug, what normally happens if they fail to teach a dog to play fetch is... nothing. The dog is not frightened of the ball, the trainer, or the game; he just doesn't fetch.

Choose your Fetch Object

The first step is to find the right ball or fetch toy for your dog. This tends to be as much about trial and error as any real science. However, we have a few guidelines which will serve you well.

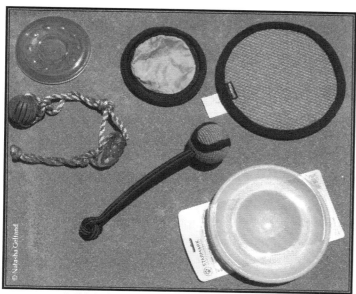

Which fetch toy makes sense for your dog?

Smaller, softer balls are usually more motivating for beginning fetchers, but you should experiment until you find objects that you are comfortable with and that your dog seems to enjoy. Try not to let your dog develop a specific favorite; fetch is more useful in training if you can use whatever object is at hand and still create an enthusiastic game. For that reason, you should use a variety of sizes, shapes, and materials for fetch objects.

Avoid toys that make noise or that have a satisfying mouth feel. Chewy, squeaky, or crunchy toys tend to be self-reinforcing, which means your dog is likely to find more satisfaction in chewing them rather than bringing them back to you. Of course, these toys might be exactly what you need if your dog has no interest in picking things up! If you use these kinds of toys to encourage your dog to learn to play fetch, try to transition off them as soon as possible.

If you have a dog who struggles to release objects cleanly, avoid balls with strings. Holding the string when you ask the dog to release makes the ball bounce in the air. This causes many dogs to try to rebite the ball - a recipe for bitten fingers and irritated trainers! If you choose to use a ball with a rope, when you ask for the release, place your hands on the ball in the dog's mouth, do not pull on the toy yourself. This will avoid turning the release into a tug game, which you do not want.

Avoid balls with strings if your dog struggles to release cleanly.

Developing Interest in Fetch

If possible, begin your fetch training indoors in a VERY dull space with as few distractions as possible. There should be no other dogs present, and nothing unusual to look at or investigate. Smaller spaces are almost always better for puppies because they are so easily distracted. Older dogs have better attention skills, so you can be a bit more flexible in your choice of location.

Next, encourage the dog to visually track the object. We recommend using a ball because they tend to be more attractive than objects that do not roll. Encourage your dog to sit on your lap (if he fits – if he doesn't, hold him back by the chest or collar), and then roll the ball away from him. If you're working with a puppy, remember that his visual tracking skills are not fully mature yet, so roll the ball slowly. An older pup or an adult dog might be more interested in faster moving objects, so zip that ball right past his nose or make it ricochet off the wall!

Don't worry if your dog chooses to sit on your lap watching quietly for awhile. Curiosity often takes over, so be patient. Try rolling the ball back and forth in front of you or bouncing it just a few inches off the ground near your dog. And remember dogs tend to focus where we focus, so focus on the object, not your pup.

When your dog shows interest in moving towards the ball, let him go! Try to stay quiet

Gently hold your dog back by the body or collar as you roll the ball.

When he is focused, let him go!

as he approaches it. Some dogs will pick it up, but others will walk away after satisfying their initial curiosity by sniffing or nosing at it. If your dog is in the latter category, go ahead fetch the ball yourself, run back to your starting point, and talk enthusiastically to the ball until your dog comes over to see what you're so excited about. Cheerfully return him to your lap, restrain him lightly, and roll the ball out again. You might find that the first few lessons involve the trainer doing a lot of fetching while the dog watches – that's okay! Quit after a few repetitions; you can always do more on another day!

Picking Up the Ball

If your puppy does not pick up the ball, try rolling it under furniture or other unusual places. This often intrigues the dog, causing him to try to get it back out again. When he does, he may not bring it back, but praise his effort anyway!

Now, simply wait to see what decision he makes next. Don't go towards your dog; let him sit alone for a short period of time. Remain quiet when he is sitting alone or moving away from you, and start praising him as he picks up the ball, or if he either looks at you or moves in your direction. If he abandons the ball, walk over, pick it up, and try again. If he settles in for a nice long chew instead, then you can go to him and gently pet him without touching the ball. You want him to associate your approach with company as opposed to thievery.

Be thoughtful about your praise. You want to project enthusiastic energy for the game without being frantic or overwhelmingly loud. Over the course of your working career together, you'll need to know what tone of voice to use and how much energy you

Praising your dog as he picks up the ball will cause him to re-orient in your direction.

If your puppy wants to chew the fetch object instead of returning to you, simply keep him company.

should project to best encourage your dog. You need to find the level of enthusiasm and excitement that is not too much or too little, but rather, just right – we call this the Goldilocks effect – and this is a great time to experiment and find out what works best for your dog.

Retrieving the Ball

The first time your pup brings the ball back to you, celebrate! This is awesome! Encourage him to sit on your lap while you pet him and admire his fine toy. Do NOT take the ball away from him. He has not yet learned the game of fetch; he is simply showing you what he has, not offering it to you so you can throw it again. When you take a fetch toy away from your dog after he returns, the unintended message is that you are not to be trusted with his valuable objects.

Most puppies have very short attention spans, so just wait for him to put the toy down. When he does, pick it up, bounce it, or roll it back and forth in front of you. Once the pup is watching carefully, give the ball another toss. If your dog is older, you'll need to be more patient; most adults

When your puppy puts the toy down, you can throw it again.

choose to possess the object much longer because they have the ability to show more sustained attention.

Quit after a few repetitions. It's better to make this a fun game to look forward to rather than something that feels like an obligation or expectation.

Teach a Release

Once your dog is regularly chasing the toy, picking it up, and coming back to sit with you, you should notice a change in your dog: he should start to value chasing the toy more than sitting and chewing on it. At this point you can offer your hand; most dogs quickly figure out this very human way of asking for something. If you have done your initial work properly and have not stolen the toy, the pup should know that your intention is to throw the toy again. So throw it! Do not pause before you throw it because this delay may be seen as teasing or punishment; as soon as the ball hits your hand, throw it back out again!

Add a release cue when your puppy is willingly releasing the toy in anticipation of another throw.

If your dog turns his head away when you reach out your hand, simply move backwards slightly to take the pressure off and wait a short period of time before trying again. The dog must understand that you will not chase him or take the ball away. He must voluntarily give it to you. If you force him, he will likely develop a game of "catch me if you can" – a game you do not want to play! When puppies discover how fun it is to be chased, it wrecks your chances of getting a good release and wreaks havoc on your recall.

When your puppy is returning to you and willingly giving up the toy for another toss, start adding a release cue.

The Importance of Generalization

Dogs have many interests, and you and your toys are often only one of them. When you first take your dog on the road to play fetch, start small. Begin in your own yard or another area that is relatively free of distractions and be prepared to make the game easier if needed. Most dogs quickly figure out that this is the same game they were playing in the house. Soon you may find yourself with an obsessive dog who lives to play fetch. Use that to your advantage in training!

Conclusion

At this point, we hope you have a dog who enjoys fetching. If you don't, read on! The next chapter is dedicated to help you problem solve a less-than-ideal game of fetch.

Chapter Twelve
Problem Solving Your Fetch Game

When the game doesn't go as planned, it's time to problem solve!

When playing fetch, ideally your dog will exhibit self-control yet still have the ability and desire to spring forward after the ball at a moment's notice. He will run after the ball as fast as he can without sightseeing, sniffing, or otherwise being distracted. He will pick up the ball instantly, wheel around as fast as possible, and drive back to the handler at maximum speed. Then, after delivering the ball to his trainer's hand, he'll be ready to start the game all over again!

Unfortunately, very few dogs actually fit this description! Most dogs have a little too much of one quality (like a desire to possess) and not enough of another (like a love of chasing prey). As a result, many teams will find that their game of fetch is unbalanced and therefore not useful for training. Luckily, fetch can be trained. In this chapter, we will present the most common problems that dogs present when learning fetch and give you the tools you need to fine tune your game.

Dog Has No Interest in Chasing the Ball

If you've followed the suggestions in the prior chapter for encouraging fetch and your dog still isn't interested in chasing the ball, it's time to up the ante. Here are our favorite ways to create interest:

Get excited about the ball yourself!

Lachie finds the ball under the couch irresistible!

Chase the ball yourself! The more excited and enthusiastic you can be about the toy, the more likely it is that your dog will show energy for it. Remember to focus on the object, not on your dog! Over time, your dog's curiosity may get the best of him and he'll decide to join the game.

Sometimes a dog's hunt drive (use of his nose) is stronger than his prey interest, so play to that strength. Start by restraining your dog by his collar. Then show your dog the ball and roll or throw it so it goes out of sight. When you release your dog, both of you should run together towards the direction where it was last seen. Encourage your dog to help you look for it. When you find it, be excited and enthusiastic, but don't pick it up; see if your dog will help you instead.

If you have access to another dog who enjoys the game of fetch, place your trainee in a crate nearby so he can watch but not participate while you engage in a lively game of fetch with the experienced player. After a brief period of time, allow your trainee to try again. Do NOT have the retriever present while the non-retriever attempts the game; this almost always intimidates the new trainee and it's very likely that you will create a non-player who simply chases the other dog - not the game we had in mind!

Sometimes when we try a new game, we give up after only two or three tries, but that truly is not enough time for interest in the game to develop. Short sessions of no more than a minute or two, once or twice a day, are the key to success in all training! Some dogs take weeks or months of effort to develop their love of the game, so don't give up too soon.

Finally, consider the environment. Is there ANYTHING else going on that might be catching your dog's eye? Training fetch in the middle of a smelly, grassy field isn't likely to be conducive to a focused game of fetch with any dog, let alone a less-driven dog. Remove all other dogs, kids, toys, and distractions when you work together.

Only play fetch in a group of dogs after each dog will happily play on his own.

Dog Has Insufficient Speed Towards the Ball

The first thing to try is holding your dog back by the chest or collar when you throw the ball. This takes advantage of the opposition reflex, a phenomenon in which your dog actually moves towards pressure. When you feel him resisting your pressure, let go!

Holding a dog back builds his drive to go forward!

If his speed is still lackluster, take off after the ball as quickly as YOU can. Most dogs have a competitive spirit and will drive forward in order to win the race! If your dog passes you as you sprint to the ball, stop running forward. If you continue to race when you are behind the dog, it's quite likely that he will feel like you are chasing him down and will defer to you by allowing you to get there first. That defeats the purpose of this exercise!

Dog Chases the Ball, but Won't Pick it Up

Here's another great opportunity to use the opposition reflex! This time, we'll restrain the dog by putting him on leash (a harness is recommended as well). Encourage him to chase the ball, but use the leash to keep him a few inches away from it. Then move the toy away again. This will increase frustration and create a greater desire to possess the ball. After several repetitions of this, allow him to grab the ball. When he does, cheer, praise, and pet him but DO NOT take the ball away.

If this does not create enough interest so that he grabs the ball, you can clicker train a general retrieve on any object and apply that to the ball. After throwing the ball, use your clicker trained fetch cue to encourage a pickup. If you're not sure how to shape a retrieve, please refer back to our book "Dog Sports Skills 1: Building Engagement and Relationship" to gain a better understanding of shaping as a training method.

Preventing the pick-up with the leash and harness makes him want it more!

Dog Picks the Ball Up but Doesn't Return

This problem is common; many dogs aren't sure they want to share their prize. Be patient. Do NOT have other dogs present since that will intimidate most dogs, causing them to fail to return. It's okay to trade for food at first, but eventually you want the dog to return the ball because he loves playing, not because he wants a cookie.

It's often advantageous to encourage him to chase you instead of trying to get him to give up the ball. Not only does chasing you encourage him to move towards you, it is also much more likely that when you stop he'll give you the ball. This requires a larger space where you can run away from your dog. You should run for at least ten seconds before you stop. If you only run far enough to get the dog close enough that you can try and grab it, he will learn to keep his distance, even during the chase.

If this doesn't work, try sitting on a comfortable dog bed or blanket in a bare room

Geneva isn't sure she wants to share her toy.

Havoc chases his trainer to build desire to return.

while you play. Many dogs will decide to sit with you in this attractive spot rather than staying away on a hard and uncomfortable floor. Remember not to steal the ball from the dog – simply spend time together until your dog shows a willingness to share with you.

Worst case scenario: play on leash, or leash the toy! Try to only use the leash to prevent the dog from leaving rather than to reel him in. Remember not to remove the object from the dog's mouth; some dogs will return when they realize you don't plan on taking it away.

Finally, don't forget about the Two Toy game we described earlier in this book. If you show your dog a second ball after he's picked up the first, he is likely to move back in your direction. Throw the second ball in the opposite direction as he approaches. Most dogs will drop the first ball as they run for the other one. Pick up the first ball. As your pup fetches the second ball, encourage a return by showing the other ball. This creates a game where you are in the middle as your dog runs out to a ball in opposite directions.

Consider either playing on leash, or putting a line on the toy itself!

To refine this game, begin waiting longer before showing your puppy the other toy.

Habit should cause him to move in your direction. Your goal will be to build up to the point where the dog drops the first toy at your feet before you show him the second toy.

If your puppy enjoys both tug and fetch, you can play this game with different objects, like a ball and a tug. As your dog returns with the ball, take out your tug toy and start playing enthusiastically at your feet. When your puppy drops the ball to grab the tug, you can pick up the ball while you continue to play with your dog. After a period of time, stop tugging and wait for a release (or ask for one if your puppy already has this behavior). Then throw the ball. Repeat with as many toys and objects as you wish. This game has the added benefit of teaching your puppy that the value of a toy is in the interaction with the trainer, not in owning it.

Dog Fetches but Has No Energy

Some dogs play fetch but seem disinterested in the game. There are two main reasons for this. First, the dog may simply be low in prey interest. Second, the dog learned to play fetch through shaping and is therefore performing only for the cookie at the end, not because he's actually interested in the game. Either way, the methods for fixing this are the same.

Start by checking your energy. Are you excited about the game? Talking about how much fun you're going to have? Showing enthusiasm? Make sure you love the game too!

Make sure you are as engaged in the game as you want your dog to be!

Next, ask your dog to perform a behavior that requires energy before throwing the ball. Good choices include bouncing or spinning on cue, but any behavior that creates movement will work. Throw the ball immediately so that you capture that forward motion. As your dog is going towards the ball, get excited! Clap and cheer. Urgently encourage him to "get it-get it-get it!"

As soon as the ball is in your dog's mouth, run away and hide. When your dog finds you, you can offer food if necessary, but make sure you throw that cookie! While the dog is running one way to grab the cookie, you should run the other way in order to put some distance between you and the dog. Watch him closely; the moment he finishes chewing and looks up, throw the ball away from him. Again, urgently encourage him to hurry for the ball. Again, as soon as his mouth is on the ball, run in the opposite direction.

Repeat this sequence as many times as you can for two minutes. If you are doing this well, you will be exhausted when your time is up! Good! This will inject your game with some much needed enthusiasm and energy.

You may need to do this for months, but it will work. Denise went through this with Brito, and his ability to play with energy and speed has increased dramatically. It took a long time, but it was worth it!

Dog Picks Up the Ball but is Slow to Return to Handler

If your dog is enthusiastic about chasing the ball, then you've done a great job of piquing his prey interest. We will take advantage of this prey interest in order to speed him up on the return. To do this, you're going to become the prey.

Throw the ball. As soon as the dog is released to fetch, turn and run in the opposite direction. When the dog picks up the ball and turns back towards you, he'll see that you are far from where he left you. Because we already know he likes the chase aspect of fetch, it should be easy to encourage him to chase you.

Erica has become the prey for Edge!

As you notice an increase in your dog's speed, start to vary the point at which you take off running in the other direction; sometimes you'll start running as soon as you release the dog to fetch the ball, while other times you'll wait until the dog is relatively close to you on the return. You want him to think you might run away at any moment, even when it appears that you are simply standing there quietly - until you explode away!

A variation on this game is the Two Toy game described previously, except the dog will chase a second ball instead of you. Be sure that you throw the toy in the opposite direction; throwing it in the direction of the dog will actually encourage him to stay back rather than driving all the way in. At first you'll want to throw the second ball immediately - this creates a fast spin on pick-up and encourages the dog to come directly back because he realizes you are going to throw the second ball in the opposite direction. Initially many dogs carry the first ball all the way to the second, so while mastering this game it's a good idea to throw the balls shorter distances so you don't spend so much time collecting them. Another option would be to have several balls with you and collect all of the extras at once.

This handler has several more discs ready to go to encourage Flash to turn quickly back to her.

While working out the details of this game, dogs will do all sorts of interesting things! Some dogs carry the first ball to the second and collect both balls. This tends to resolve itself on its own as the dog masters the game. Some dogs carry the first ball to the second one and then stand there in confusion. In this case, verbally encourage your dog with a sense of urgency in your voice - and then cheer when he makes a decision! Yet other dogs run out to the first ball, pick it up and carry it to the second one, and then return to you with the first one. If your dog does this, just run out and pick up the second ball and start over. Time and experience tend to work out these kinks. Eventually, your dog will learn to run to the first one, carry it back towards you until he sees you pull out the second one, at which point he will spit out the first one and drive towards the second ball that is now heading the opposite direction.

Once your dog is spinning quickly in anticipation, begin to delay the throw of the second ball until he is already running back, preferably making eye contact with you. Now you will reward the dog's choice to turn quickly and run directly towards you with a throw of the second ball in the opposite direction.

Over time, this game can progress to the point that the second ball is not thrown until the dog returns all the way to you and gives you the ball. At that stage, it's easy to go to playing with one ball - simply throw the one that was returned to you. If you ever notice his speed decreasing, you can always bring back the second toy as a surprise.

The Two Toy game is also very effective for dogs who sightsee or arc on their return. By giving the dog a reason to return quickly and directly, the problem tends to diminish without any intervention from you.

Dog Returns Part Way, then Veers Off

As soon as you notice your dog veering, back up and away from where the dog is heading so that you end up further from the dog. At the same time, head in the direction of the dog's tail in order to get behind him. It's important to back away; if you move towards the dog it will look like a game of chase. Most dogs like to be chased, so be sure that when you go behind the dog you are increasing distance between the two of you. If you turn and run away after you get behind your dog's tail, you'll make him even more determined to get to you!

Denise is encouraging Lyra to come in directly by heading behind her tail and then running off to be chased!

Dog Returns but Does Not Release the Ball

Dogs who struggle to release the toy are often worried that you're going to steal it from them. Be sure that any time the ball is returned, you throw it again. This puts the focus on the game, not on possession. When you want to end the game, take the dog away from the toy – not the toy away from the dog. You can do this by holding the dog gently against your legs with one hand around his middle and the other in the collar to keep his head off the ground. Most dogs will not hold a toy in this position for more than a few minutes (and this will get shorter with time). When the ball drops from the dog's mouth, put the dog away and return for the toy later. Use a different cue from your standard release, such as "all done" or "that'll do" to teach that play time is over.

It is absolutely acceptable to trade food for a toy. Place your hand on the toy and stop moving completely. With your other hand, place a treat immediately in front of your dog's nose or actually put the treat in your dog's mouth behind the ball. Most dogs will let go of the ball to eat the treat. As soon as your dog swallows, throw the ball again. Tossing a handful of treats on the ground in front of your dog can also work to get a release. As soon as your dog eats the treats, throw the ball again. If your dog is willing to release for food, you can add a verbal release cue right before the food is presented. With repetition, your dog will start to release on cue even before you offer the food.

Trading for food is an excellent way to get your ball back. Now, throw it again quickly!

Dog Returns but Won't Deliver the Ball to the Handler's Hand

There are two reasons a dog doesn't deliver the toy to your hand.

The first is because he doesn't know what you want. These dogs bring the ball back and drop it on the ground near their handlers. Some people don't mind picking up the ball, but if you want your dog to put the ball in your hand instead, you'll need to do a bit of acting. Pretend that you are physically not capable of picking up the ball. Point at it, look sad, and encourage your dog to pick it up again – most dogs do, although it might take a few minutes the first time. When your dog picks it up, get excited and reach for it. If he drops it before you can grab the ball, once again pretend that you can't reach it. Dogs usually figure this out - although handlers often have a hard time waiting the dog out. If necessary, you may need to end a couple of training sessions with the ball on the ground because you just couldn't get it!

Riley is not about to give up a beloved ball.

The other reason dogs do not deliver the toy to your hand is because they are in conflict. They want you to throw the ball again, but they also want to own the object. We say that these dogs are possessive. Being possessive is not necessarily bad - it is often associated with dogs who are higher in drive and who truly care about objects - but it can create a challenge if you want to play an interactive game of fetch!

Denise's "escaping" body language is inviting Lyra to come forward.
At the same time she is playfully pushing her away.

Try this: Move to a smaller space and throw the ball a very short distance to keep the dog's drive and energy on the lower side. When your dog returns, gently push him back. Your body language should be playfully saying, "No, keep the ball!" but by backing up, you're suggesting that you might play if he insists. Continue to move backwards and GENTLY pushing your dog away until he's pushing back with determination. At this point, agree to take the ball and throw it immediately.

Here's another option: Throw the ball as usual, but as the dog returns, turn and walk away with your hand held out and somewhat high. This encourages your dog to jump up and give you the ball while also moving with you. Facing away from the dog will reduce the amount of pressure placed on the dog, which can reduce conflict.

Lyra at Denise's side getting ready to jump up and give her the ball!

One final option: If your dog is interested in tugging in addition to possessing a toy, switch to tug rather than fetch when he returns. Now he isn't being asked to give up the toy! This works best if you throw an object that can be tugged and you follow it up with a very weak game of tug. The desire to fight makes the dog be more willing to put the object in your hands, while your weak game of tug reduces his possessiveness. The end result is that your dog will return to play more, place the toy in your hands for a mild game of tug, and then release altogether for the chance to run and start the game over again. One word of caution, though: this is not a good option if your dog struggles to release a tug toy as it may actually increase the dog's desire to clamp down.

Dog Crashes into Handler on Return

Some dogs are so fast and enthusiastic that they literally take the handler down on their

return! This tends to be caused by handlers who are scared the dog is going to run into them and back up out of nervousness as a result. Ironically, backing up actually increases the dog's speed, making the problem worse over time.

Walking towards a dog who is too fast and enthusiastic will often cause him to give you some much needed space!

The solution is to do the opposite. As your dog is returning, start walking towards him, making sure you are facing him directly with your front. Most dogs, when they notice that you are approaching, will stop their forward trajectory to avoid a crash. After all, they might enjoy crashing into you, but they don't want you to crash into them!

After a few days of walking directly at your dog, start waiting a little longer to move towards him. Do this gradually until your dog is only five or ten feet away before you start moving.

Dog Struggles to Fetch a Tug Toy

While we normally think of fetch as a game that uses a ball, it is not uncommon that we will want our dogs to fetch a tug toy as well. This tends to cause a dilemma for many dogs. With a ball, the dog knows that you will throw it again. With a tug toy, though, dogs are expecting a fight to ensue. This can bring about conflict if the dog does not feel up to the task. As a result, some dogs go out and pick up the tug but appear reluctant to bring the toy back – even though they do this just fine with a ball!

To combat this, throw a tug object (preferably a training toy rather than a drive-building toy), and when the dog returns, simply ask for a release and throw the toy immediately. If the dog does not return, go and sit with him, but do not touch the object. Wait for him to drop it on his own, then quickly pick it up and throw it again. This will go faster if you use an object that isn't much fun to chew.

When your dog is confidently returning with his tug toy expecting another game of fetch, the next step is to ask for a release and follow it with only two seconds of tug. Ask for another release, and then throw the toy. Work your way up to having your dog bring the toy back, tug directly, and then release for another throw. Take your time! It's worth working through this sequence so that you have the option of letting your dog win tug objects on occasion without struggling to get the dog to bring them back.

Some dogs struggle to fetch a tug toy.

Conclusion

Playing fetch is a wonderful game for you and your canine companion. In addition to exercise and general bonding, it is also an excellent training tool. Rewards can be delivered in a timely fashion even if you are far away. Most dogs can learn to truly enjoy playing the game, even if they aren't avid retrievers by nature. If you make a point of using a variety of objects, the game can include tug toys as well as balls or ring objects such as dumbbells.

Now go out and have a ball!

Chapter Thirteen
Introduction to Personal Play

Personal play is a true gift in the competition ring!

What happens to your training when you don't have any toys handy? Or when you run out of food? Or - and we suspect this will happen to you since you're reading this book - when you step in a competition ring? How will you reward your dog when you have nothing but your personality and the strength of your relationship?

One answer is personal play. This chapter will introduce you to the basics of what personal play is and why it is so beneficial (and the benefits go beyond simply standing in as a reinforcer). Then, subsequent chapters will explain how you and your dog can learn to engage in this very exciting form of play. We'll also discuss advanced games you can play together and do some problem-solving for the most common personal play problems.

What is Personal Play?

Personal play is a form of play that occurs just between you and your dog. No toys, no balls, no food. All of the interaction occurs directly between the two of you with no intermediary. This skill is difficult to master because each dog is a unique individual; there is no one size fits all formula.

Personal play can be hard to learn since we tend to have a hard time relaxing and letting go, especially when it comes to "serious" ventures like dog sports or performing in front of others. Acting silly with our dogs is not considered to be a grown-up thing to do. And while Denise has noticed that women do not consider silly crazy play to be a feminine behavior, Deb has noticed that men do not consider it to be very masculine either. So let's just say that personal play is usually difficult for adult trainers.

Not surprisingly, both children and puppies take to personal play much more naturally than adults of either species. Children run, laugh, and roll on the ground, often all in quick succession… and so do puppies! In fact, puppies take to personal play with humans so well that the easiest way to learn this skill is to practice with a puppy before trying it with your adult dog.

Like humans, dogs can lose the skills of play if they do not practice them as they mature. That doesn't mean you cannot bring the interest back, but you'll have to work harder and more thoughtfully to bring out your dog's playful side - not to mention your own!

Children naturally gravitate towards playing with dogs.

Why We Do It

Personal play has a tremendous range of benefits for both the dog and the trainer. Teams engaged in personal play almost always generate a good deal of shared energy. Rather than a dog leaping and jumping alone, the team is leaping and jumping together! This energy is trainer focused and therefore highly usable; it's an excellent physical, mental, and emotional state for the dog to be in during training.

Personal play encourages natural handler focus. When a dog is not sure what you are going to do next, he tends to pay attention simply because you are interesting. If a trainer heels in a traditional fashion for 45 seconds, and then suddenly tags her dog and runs off to the right, most dogs will start watching carefully with a cheerful, expectant attitude.

Likewise, these games can be combined with exercises that the dog finds a bit dull, such as the slow pace of heeling. If you routinely pair slow heeling with an explosive play release, you'll soon find your previously uninspired heeler paying extremely good attention with an excellent attitude.

One of our favorite uses of personal play is to reduce the use of classic food and object based rewards. This is particularly valuable if you participate in dog sports where routines can be long and food and toys are not allowed. Once the dog has learned that classic rewards will not come in a trial environment, personal play can get a dog through an eight or ten minute obedience routine. Just small bits – a few seconds between exercises – can be enough to keep a dog engaged and motivated.

Dogs naturally pay attention to us when we are being playful.

Personal play relieves stress. When both members of the team are engaged with each other, smiling and laughing, it's hard to be nervous. On the flip side, when a team that can normally play well together is unable to do so, it is also an excellent barometer of distress. It is possible that something needs to be done to help the dog (or trainer) feel more comfortable in that specific environment.

And finally, personal play with dogs is simply fun! Few adults feel they have permission to run around and be silly. Now you not only have permission, you are being encouraged to do it! If you aren't smiling, laughing, clapping, and being a little bit goofy, it's time to work on your skills in this area a bit more. If this sounds very uncomfortable for you, start slowly. You don't have to become crazy to have a good time, and you certainly don't have to do it in public. But you will have to give yourself permission to start the process.

Trainer, Meet Dog

There is one more reason we think personal play is great, and it's so important that it deserves its own section. Personal play encourages a deeply intimate relationship with your dog. Not only will you enjoy spending time together, but you'll really begin to understand just what it is that makes your dog tick. You'll learn about his likes and dislikes, his preferences, and you'll gain a much deeper understanding of his personality. Of course, there are many ways to develop this kind of relationship, but personal play will help you learn about aspects of your dog in ways nothing else can.

Personal play has no rules beyond mutual enjoyment, which frees both you and your dog up to be creative in the way you interact. Some dogs love to play foot games, where you reach out and pretend to grab their feet (or take hold very gently). Some dogs love face squishing games, where you grab their heads. Some dogs enjoy light pushing and shoving, while other dogs do not want to be touched but love to come into your space. Because personal play is so customizable, trainers can spends months or years learning how to best engage their dogs – an enjoyable process for those of us who really value our canine relationships.

There is no "right" way to play with your dog!

The highly individual nature of personal play means that trainers who appreciate personal play spend a good deal of time simply studying their dogs, watching interactions with children, strangers, and other dogs. This time spent watching your dog is excellent both for general relationship building and also for finding the keys to engage your dog's playfulness.

There are many things that you might see when you're watching your dog. Does he tend to chase when playing with other dogs? Then look for games that relate to chase: chase the ball, chase the food, chase the human! Does your dog like to pretend fight? Then look for games that relate to fight: fight the tug, fight to get to the food, wrestle (fight) the human! Does your dog like to be chased? Then look for games where your dog is the prey: pretend he is a rabbit, grab him, and let him leap away!

You'll also learn which aspects of the prey sequence - eye, stalk, chase, catch, kill - are strongest and weakest for your dog because most dogs spend a lot of time in whatever part of that sequence is most important to them. This makes sense because play is basically a suspension of reality. Your dog knows that he's not really chasing or catching a rabbit when you throw a ball, and he knows that when he wrestles with you, his goal is not to take you down to kill and eat. But just like humans, dogs like to pretend, too.

If you think about it, dogs play the same games that we humans do. We play chase, tug of war, hide and seek, and wrestling games. We engage in mental contests with one another. And we have the same problems; sometimes when we wrestle with another person, we get hurt and flip into anger or aggression. Or one player gets too rough and the other decides to leave the game. Play can help both humans and dogs learn to control their arousal levels and play by the rules.

Conclusion

Learning personal play is not easy. It takes time, mechanical skills, and studying your partner to get it right. And the learning is really never done. Because personal play is so highly individual to each player, you may master it with one dog but need to learn again with another. So is it worth it to put in the time and find a route to personal play that works for your dog? The answer is a resounding yes! When you see your dog visibly brighten in your presence and show delight in your playful company, it's hard not to see the value.

What is your dog's natural style with other dogs?

Chapter Fourteen
Teaching (and Learning) Personal Play

Dogs (and people!) come hard-wired with basic play skills. These skills are designed to allow a dog or a human to practice being a predator, and all of the games that dogs or people play with each other are simply modified versions of real hunting skills. Hide and seek allows the dog to practice finding prey. Chase games like tag are a version of prey pursuit. Wrestling mimics taking down prey. "Bitey face" games mimic a killing bite.

These hard-wired play skills also tend to rely on the senses, especially those of sight, sound, and touch. Dogs are highly visual and identify small motions, quick snaps, and stalking behaviors as play. Sound also stimulates a dog's auditory prey response, especially high-pitched squeaking noises. The sense of touch – pushing, wrestling, and rolling - engages the dog's sense of fight.

This chapter will focus on using the senses to create a make believe version of hunting. As you read, think about how your dog plays and how you can mimic that.

You can learn quite a bit about play by watching dogs play with each other. What is your dog's natural style?

What Would Rover Do?

If you watch play among dogs, you'll notice a few things. First, different individuals prefer different play styles. Some want to chase (predator) and others want to be chased (prey). Some don't run at all, preferring to wrestle and practice the fight or kill portion of the prey sequence. When two individuals with significantly different styles come together, they either modify their preferences to accommodate the other, or they find a new playmate. It's no surprise that dogs have preferences about who they want to play with!

You'll also notice that in the vast majority of play interactions, there is significant give and take. Each partner will likely reverse roles regularly. It is unusual for one dog to always be the predator while the other is always the prey. Dogs tend to take turns so each can be the aggressor at different times. This is vital to remember when you're playing with your dog. If you remember that almost all play is based on being a pretend predator or prey, then you'll also recognize how important it is to take turns! The softer and more sensitive your dog, the more often you need to be the prey in order to build up your dog's confidence! If your dog is harder or stronger by temperament, he may well enjoy a good wrestling match on the ground!

Another thing you will notice is how dogs take frequent breaks in the middle of their play. These breaks often include distinct calming signals such as abruptly turning away to sniff, shaking from head to tail, or acting completely disinterested – only to start all over again within a few seconds or a minute. These breaks appear to serve as a mechanism to both prevent over arousal and to de-escalate the situation if one of the dogs starts to play too roughly.

Finally, it's worth noticing how much play is stylized and predictable. Let's consider two common scenarios to illustrate this point; the first will end in a wrestling match and the second in a game of chase.

SCENARIO 1:
Dog A wants to play with Dog B, and initiates a game by crouching and stalking closer to the victim. When Dog B notices Dog A, he stops what he's doing to watch carefully. Dog A, sure that she has Dog B's attention, suddenly rushes towards Dog B. The game is on! This sequence, in which one dog invites the other to play and the other responds, is predictable.

SCENARIO 2:
Dog A wants to play a game of chase with Dog B, so she stands five feet away from him, barks sharply several times, and waits for a response. When Dog B looks at her, Dog A offers a fast play bow in invitation. Dog B reciprocates and Dog A takes off running, taking on the role of prey while Dog B follows in hot pursuit! Although it's a different game, this sequence is also predictable – there is an invitation and a response.

If you study dogs playing and learn some of the rituals that dogs (especially your own dog) use during play, it will be easier for you to communicate with your dog in a way that he will understand.

Getting Started: Expression

One of the easiest ways to get started in personal play is to change your facial expression to be more open and welcoming. Tilt your head slightly to one side, smile, open your eyes wide, and make a little sound to attract attention. Continue smiling and verbally encourage the dog to come over for a visit. If this expression feels familiar, it should; it is the same expression that adults use when greeting a child they don't know. It is not noisy, intense, or demanding; you are simply showing the dog that you are a friendly and kind person who wants to interact with him.

Make sure you have a welcoming expression!

If your dog does not react positively to this invitation, you can try further altering a few aspects of your expression. Smile without showing your teeth. Turn your face slightly away from your dog rather than facing him straight on. Blink a few times. Turn your back on your dog and make squeaking noises at your toes – and do not look to see how your dog responds! You need to reduce the pressure on your dog.

Dogs differ widely in their reactions based on past experiences and temperament, so be ready to experiment until your dog reacts with interest and engagement. Once your dog acknowledges your welcoming expression, you can work on getting your dog into a playful state of mind.

Auditory Cues

If you haven't already, it's time to add some auditory cues to let your dog know you'd like to play. Auditory cues, or noises that we make to attract attention, should be fairly quiet. We do this both because when you are quiet your dog will have to listen carefully to hear you, and because high volume noises are often scary as opposed to inviting.

What really matters when it comes to auditory cues is the tone of your voice. Squeaky voices are appealing, especially when combined with wide eyes and big smiles. Hissing sounds – like a snake – can attract your dog's attention, but they are also usually perceived as threatening. Therefore, when you use a hissing sound, you must move quickly away from your dog to make it clear that you are willing to play the role of prey, not predator. Other sounds that tend to be attention getting are "tsch tsch" and "pup pup pup!" The latter is common among breeders when calling to their litters, and it's amazing how many puppies remember this from their youngest days and respond enthusiastically! You'll need to experiment to find just the right sounds for your dog.

Auditory cues will be very important when you enter competitions, so make sure you use them and combine them with any play-based moves that work for you. Soon, simply looking at your dog and saying something like "tsch tsch!" will cause him to explode with energy that can be used in the ring.

Visual Cues: Body Posture

If your dog has shown interest in interacting with you based on your facial expression and auditory cues, add in a change of body posture to see if you can elicit some actual play. Be careful not to face your dog head on; frontal approaches are often seen as aggressive moves. Instead, significantly drop your overall height so that you look like you are crouching slightly and about to do something interesting. As a matter of fact, you ARE about to do something interesting, and we want your posture to predict that!

If you watch wolves or dogs hunting, you'll notice that they stop forward movement, eye the prey, and drop down into a lowered body position. If you watch dogs playing, you'll often see this same behavior as part of an initiation of a game. The same thing happens when you play tag with a child.

Dogs lower their position when they want to initiate play. You should too!

A lowered body posture with more of your side to the dog than your front communicates that something is going to happen without being threatening.

Visual Cues: Movement

Things start to get very interesting about now. Your dog should be watching you intently, probably with a closed mouth. If so, snap your body away from your dog, run a small distance away, and call to your dog in a happy voice at the same time. Make sure you are smiling and inviting, but continue to face AWAY from your dog – remember, you are escaping prey!

Hopefully your dog jumped up and chased after you, tail wagging. Praise, laugh, and pat him... and then do it again! Stop moving. Lower your body position. Suddenly snap and run away from your dog, until he quickly chases after you and catches you. Repeat! Remember, it is extremely important that you turn away from your dog – that means you will not be able to see your dog's response except with your peripheral vision or when he shows up next to you. You should be looking down at your toes, talking in an excited tone of voice, hoping he'll show up.

Does your dog like movement?

Practice this sequence until your dog begins to pay attention to you when you stop moving and start to lower your body. You want your lowered stalking posture to predict the game of chase for your dog. If you keep that association strong, your dog will learn to pay better attention to you when you are quiet and still. Being able to get your dog's attention without becoming noisy, especially in public settings, can be quite an advantage.

Once your dog comes running with wide eyes and an open mouthed expression, go ahead and run a little further, using your auditory cues (laughing! clapping! giggling!) to encourage your dog to chase you. Often, running around a table or another solid object works better than running away in a straight line because it equalizes your speed and gives you an advantage. Dogs are much faster than humans in a straight line and will catch you almost instantly. Also, it's hard not to laugh as you run around a table with your dog trying to catch you!

You can also play this game around corners in your house. Just barely enter the room your dog is in and go into your stalking posture to gain his attention. When your dog notices you, turn and disappear around the corner into another room, calling and laughing. Most dogs will race in to see what you're up to! Praise and interact physically!

Another option is to start your game in one room, race to a bedroom, and then leap onto the bed or behind it. Hiding and then popping out as the dog comes near simulates a predator ambushing his prey, which causes some dogs to get giddy with excitement!

When your dog catches up, you can either pet him, thump him on the side, let him leap up at you, roll on the ground together, or gently push him and run away again. It's also fine to sit on the ground and let your dog lick you while you laugh hysterically, if that's what you both enjoy. There are no rules other than you should both be having fun.

Physical Touch

Physical touch can be a great addition to chase games. One way to start doing this is to gently push your dog away, either on his chest or on his side. In either case, you should move away from your dog. A chest push should cause you to snap backwards and away. A side push should cause you to turn away completely and allow the dog to move into your space. With experience, you can stand still and face your dog while you push him gently in various directions.

Watch to be sure that your dog is enjoying the experience. As long as your dog continues to comfortably and reliably move back into your space, you're fine to continue playing. If your dog ever moves away and stays away, or if he shows any classic avoidance behaviors (sniffing, head turned away, stops moving, lip licking, and so on), then you have accidentally confused your play signals with aggression. Slow down, take a break, or switch to vigorous patting or thumping on his sides and chest instead.

This sequence shows Erica using opposition reflex followed by chase in her play with Edge.
Opposition reflex play is a great use of physical touch!

Conclusion

The most common mistake trainers make in these beginning stages is being intimidating. Once you offer a play based behavior, you must turn away to reduce frontal pressure and then quickly move away to allow your dog the choice to come back into your space. This builds confidence and makes play into a proper game of give and take. You offered to play, and now the dog may freely accept your offer and make the next move. With time and confidence, it's fine to go directly into more confrontational play like wrestling, but that's not the best place to start.

Always reevaluate what you are doing and how it is working so you can get the most benefit and enjoyment out of your play sessions. When looking for play moves that appeal to your dog, take a hard look at your dog's style when playing with food or toys. Most dogs have a preferred style; for example, if your dog loves toy games that involve fight, then it is likely that your dog will enjoy opposition reflex games (pushing away), wrestling, and leg or foot grabbing.

Chapter Fifteen
Advanced Personal Play

Now that you understand the basics of personal play, it's time to build on your skills. In this chapter, we'll discuss a number of games that you can play with your dog. They come in three main types: Movement Games, Touch Games, and Play as Personal Approval. Of course, there is plenty of overlap in each of these categories.

As you read, please remember that these games are suggestions only. The only rule with personal play is that you BOTH should be having fun. This is especially important to remember as a number of these games involve active physical interaction. If your dog has any issues with touch or vigorous play, it is your responsibility to alter these games according to your dog's needs. The same goes for you - alter them to accommodate any physical limitations you may have. What's most important is the attitude of fun and excitement you bring to your play. If both of you aren't having a great time, then either you need to change something about the way you are playing the game, or find a different game that suits both of you better.

Movement Games

Movement games are those that do not require hands-on play. For example, these tend to be games of chase rather than wrestling. If your dog is not comfortable with physical contact during play, it is worth building up his tolerance for physical play, but it is absolutely NOT necessary for excellent play interactions.

What follows are some types of movements you can incorporate into your play repertoire rather than actual games - but you should still have fun!

Quick Changes of Direction

Dogs can move faster than we humans can when running in a straight line. To increase the challenge (and the fun!) for our dogs, we can make quick changes of direction. Now simply catching up to you isn't enough; your dog must also follow your zigging and zagging. Using obstacles like tables and chairs will also give you a chance to get away. Don't be limited by your feet - crawling around on the floor under a table with your dog is sure to put both you and your dog in a playful state of mind.

Movement games tend to be games of chase. Kalie loves chasing Jeff!

Using an obstacle gives Jeff a much needed advantage!

Changes of direction can be combined with auditory cues and physical touch. For example, give your dog a verbal cue that something interesting is going to happen, slow your movement and drop your posture to a semi-stalking position, lightly push your dog's neck area, and zip away from the dog as fast as you can! When the dog almost catches up, jump behind a chair or run around a table, and wrestle with your dog when you get caught! While this entire interaction might take less than ten seconds, it's a whole lot of fun for both of you.

Give a slight push on the neck and...run away!

Vertical Movement

Adding vertical movement to your play session allows for a lot more physical exertion from the dog – and less for you. Trust us, after a minute of active play, you'll be grateful for any breaks that you can get!

High hand touches followed by running away!

To encourage vertical movement, ask your dog to perform a hand touch, preferably as high up in the air as your dog can comfortably go. Once your dog jumps, take that split second when he is in the air to run away. This is especially effective if you do it while your dog is moving with you in heel or side position. Your dog never knows when the game is coming, which encourages a good deal of natural focus.

You can alternate between hand touches, work, and games of chase all in quick succession! Try a hand touch followed by heeling at a fast pace, or a hand touch to a quick down. Then go back to a game of chase after the touch. The great variety of possibilities helps to keep your dog engaged and guessing about what might happen next.

Jumping on the Trainer

Some dogs enjoy jumping on their trainers. Of course, it is completely up to you to decide if this is acceptable or not. If you are comfortable with your dog jumping onto your body, go ahead and pat your leg or chest (depending on the size of your dog) with a cheerful "up" cue. Or simply throw your hands up in the air! Most dogs figure this out right away unless you have discouraged jumping up.

Most dogs enjoy jumping on their trainers. It's up to you to decide if that is something you want to allow.

Hands up is usually interpreted as permission to jump up.

Now combine it with play or work. After your dog catches up to you, encourage him to jump on you. Tell him how smart he is; pet his furry head and thump his sides. Give a nice hug to dogs who enjoy close personal contact.

When you are ready to resume play or work, try getting very quiet for a second or two, and then snap backwards into work or play! Soon, your quiet demeanor followed by a quick snap will be associated with something interesting happening and your dog will quickly resume more active play or active work, depending on what you have in mind.

Leaping in the Air

For those of you who don't want your dogs jumping on you, consider encouraging your dog to leap around you without touching you. This makes sense for larger dogs or for handlers with balance problems or who are physically frail.

The easiest way to encourage leaping is with a simple hand touch. Start small by asking for a very easy hand touch a few inches above the dog's head and off to your side. If you alternate hands and sides, most dogs will naturally keep their feet off you because they are focused on jumping back and forth between your hands. Over time, raise your expectations until a high hand touch requires serious commitment and thought from your dog. The higher the hand touch, the more rewarding it will be for your dog, and the more focus it will require from your dog in order to complete it successfully. If you can get a good hand touch from your side, encourage the same basic behavior from the front. Try two hands up in front of your body to encourage your dog to jump straight up in front but not to land on you.

Now let's add a chase element! As your dog targets your hand for a touch, move it quickly backwards so the dog falls short. Laugh and offer it again in a new position! Most dogs start diving at your hands with total commitment until they actually connect. When your dog hits one hand touch, quickly put that hand away and offer the other hand – in any position you like – for the next one. You can alternate one hand low and the other hand high. For added interest, move backwards, sideways, or turn in circles as you offer hand touches at different heights and in different positions. The games are on!

Gus is too big to jump on his trainer, but he can still jump in the air!

Denise and Polly are playing with hand touches offered in all sorts of positions - Polly needs to be quick!

Spinning

Quick spins allow a dog to release energy in the midst of play. This will require that you pre-teach the "spin" cue. If you're not sure how to do this, please refer to the section on tricks in Book 1.

Get your dog moving and chasing you. When your dog is well engaged, ask for a quick spin to the left or right. Follow this with a hand touch up high or take off running! This will encourage fast motion and more energy in play.

Hide and Seek

Hide and seek is fun for both you and your dog, especially dogs who enjoy using their nose. Either place your dog on a stay, or if his stay isn't solid enough yet, have another person restrain him while you hide. Once you're in place, the dog can be released with a cheerful "Find her!" command. If your dog watched you run off, odds are good that he will figure out the game with no further effort on your part. If he isn't sure what is wanted, run back to within twenty feet of him and then dart off around a corner so that he can find you easily. This builds confidence and creates a positive association with the game.

Gemma loves to spin for her handler.

Reese is thrilled to come around the corner to find his friend!

Hide and seek can be followed up by running, chasing, spins, or wrestling on the ground. Regardless, make sure your dog feels he has accomplished something spectacular when he finds you so he'll be thrilled to play again!

Where's My Doggy?

This is an ideal game for a more withdrawn dog. To play, turn your back on your dog and start talking to your toes. Using your dog's name, say, "Where's my Doggy?"

Ivy loves to find Sue's face!

(substituting your dog's name for "doggy" of course). When your dog comes around to see you, turn away as if you were unaware that he was coming up on your side, and continue to ask your toes where your doggy is. Many dogs will either come between your legs or increase their speed as they come around you. If your dog doesn't, after 10 or 15 seconds, allow your dog to end up in your line of sight and exclaim, "There's my doggy!"

Another variation of this involves hiding your face on the ground and encouraging your dog to find you! Expect to get licked when your dog "finds" you!

Where is my Polly?
Where could she be?

Here she comes.

There's Polly!

Touch Games

In this section, we've included games that use a lot of touch. Again, if this is not comfortable for your dog, alter the game so that he's having fun. These games tend to combine a variety of moves, sounds, and noises – lots of fun!

Gonna Get Your Butt!

In this game, your goal is to tap your dog's butt. Your dog's goal is to prevent you from doing that. Obviously, if you are bigger than your dog and reach over the top of your dog, you will be able to get his butt easily, so we consider that particular move to be cheating. Instead, to get your dog's butt, you must fake him out. Reach out with your left hand as if you're going to grab him, then quickly change direction and try to get him with your right hand! This should be a tap, not a hair-pulling grab.

If you do succeed in getting his butt, tap him and run away! And if you do not succeed after a few tries, then you should snap backwards and run away anyway. Dogs love this game - and so do we!

Denise and Lyra play "Gonna Get Your Butt!" After Denise tags Lyra's butt, she runs away!

Gonna Get Your Foot

This game is easiest to play while sitting on the ground, but you can also play while standing by bending over. The goal here is to quickly grab a foot and let go - do not HOLD the foot! If you get one foot and your dog pulls it away, grab the other foot! Make a rhythm; front right followed by front left followed by front right. And just as your dog figures out the rhythm change your mind and grab a back foot instead. If you get your dog to jump away, then run off and let him get you for a change!

Try playfully grabbing your dog's foot and see what happens.

Claw Hand

Start with a calm, slow movement forward, extend your arm, and create a claw shape with your hand. Move towards your dog, slowly moving your claw fingers in and out. Just as you see your dog curl back his lips like he's going to get you, gently grab his head for just one second and then pull your hand back. Many dogs get downright giddy when they see that claw hand show up.

This is a great game to combine with work. Wait until your dog is near your side in work and then make your claw hand. If he jumps at your hand, then make your hand jump back! Your dog won that round!

Claw hand can also turn into jaw wrestling. Using either one or two hands, approach your dog's head like you're going to swallow his head with your hands. Many dogs will open their mouths to stop you; if your dog does, jaw wrestle with your dog. If you're not sure what that looks like, watch two dogs together and you'll get the idea pretty quickly!

Dogs love to pretend that they are biting your hand!

Doggy Toss

Doggy toss is a way to take a dog who is facing you and pop him through your legs from front to back or from back to front. This not only reduces the pressure from the front of your body, but it also gives your dog the opportunity to turn and come back at you. Most dogs find this to be great fun!

To do this, as your dog is facing you with his head near the space between your legs, give his butt a little push as you step forwards - now your dog is behind you. Most dogs whirl around almost instantly, at which time you should pop backwards as if you were scared of him facing you.

Denise gently "pops" Brito through her legs.

Brito gets one last gentle "pop" on his bottom.

Denise and Brito both turn towards each other.

Brito is ready for a new game!

You can also play doggy toss while sitting on the ground. Stop moving, toss your dog off your lap, and then either roll away or jump up and run away as soon as your dog lands and turns to face you.

Be gentle with this game when you introduce it. You will need to experiment to find out how hard you're going to toss your dog!

Rexy loves to wrestle with her dad!

Zoey enjoys her hand touches.

Doggy Squash

Some dogs love to be smooshed. You can give a dog a big bear hug and roll on the ground with him, or you can let the dog smash you to the ground. Regardless, you need a very trusting relationship for this game - the dog must understand that you won't really smash him, and that it is strictly for fun. Wrestling can be a great game for both dog and handler!

Hand Touches

This is a great game for a less confident player who needs rules to have a good time. This is also one of our few games in which we use cookies. To play, ask your dog to do a hand touch and reward him for doing so. Now, start alternating where you offer hand touches - left hand or right hand, low or high. Be quick! Your dog should be able to succeed, but only if he is paying very careful attention and trying hard! Feel free to reward sometimes with cookies, but reward others by running away and letting your dog chase you for successful hand touches, with or without a cookie for catching up.

Play as Personal Approval

In addition to using play as a way to build energy and excitement, play can also be used to express approval. This can also be called praise, and the purpose is to tell the dog that we love and value him whether or not he has done anything special. If your dog feels that you enjoy his company regardless of his work, he will start to seek you out. Dogs enjoy human company; this desire to interact with a human is innate and appears a few weeks after birth. The behavior of the trainer can influence how important praise is to a dog. The more you praise your dog and gently interact with him away from work, the more your dog will seek your approval.

Shasta knows that she is loved.

Play as personal approval is often calming rather than stimulating. Instead of getting the dog aroused and intense, praise allows you to bring a dog back to earth and into a more thoughtful mindset. When praise is used to calm the dog, your demeanor should mimic what you want from your dog. Your voice should be calm, soothing, and supportive. Your hands should move slowly over your dog with rhythmic patting or petting motions rather than hard thumps or pushes. Scratch his head, rub the insides of his ears, and massage his belly. Anything you do which calms the dog down and quiets his behavior is a positive praise interaction.

Griffin knows that his mom wants to be with him through their regular, playful interactions.

This type of interaction does not need to happen during training time. When your dog does something that pleases you – even if it is as simple as lying quietly at your feet while you watch TV - it's important to let him know that you appreciate his choices. This makes the behavior more likely to happen again, which makes the time you spend in your dog's company more enjoyable for both of you.

Praise is also natural to most people. Most people have dogs for the connection and company that owning a dog provides. Even if they never actively play and run with their dogs, almost all pet owners understand and use praise to develop a deeper relationship with their pets. The bond that is built is different than that which is created with rousing, energetic games of play. Praise and quiet petting provides benefits for both of you. Your dog benefits by feeling valued and important and you benefit from a decrease in pulse rate, respiration, and blood pressure. The value of personal connection, whether with another human or with your canine companion, cannot be overstated. Take advantage of this – pet and praise your dog as often as you can! It's good for both of you.

Unfortunately, sometimes dog sport competitors get so focused on creating a working dog that they forget the value of having a dog as a pet and as a companion. The dog becomes a means to an end - usually ribbons and titles. Winning is definitely fun, but when the dog becomes little more than the vehicle towards this goal, the personal relationship suffers and the benefits of companionship are lost.

Praise will build your personal and your working relationship with your dog. It can also come into the competition ring with you. Dogs will value praise more when they receive it often. Don't be stingy with genuine praise!

Be careful about when you praise your dog. If you only praise your dog when you plan to withhold a classic reward, you will actually make praise a negative marker – what a disaster! The way to make praise valuable is to use it as a regular reinforcer in daily life. Keep it separate from work at first, and then, as it gains value, use it as a possible reward for work.

If you sincerely praise your dog often in the course of daily life, it will transfer much more easily into the competition arena. Do not make the mistake of believing that all your dog cares about is food and toys. Dogs care very much about your approval, and they will work hard to earn it.

Conclusion

It's hard to overstate what a great relationship builder it can be to have a dog who will play with you, although we know it can be tough to get started. Hopefully you now have some ideas for playing with your dog, but if you need more, think about what your dog hears, sees, and feels. Consider how your dog interacts with other dogs, and always remember the predator/prey relationship. Start with just one or two games and learn about your dog's preferences. What makes him perk up his ears? What makes him walk away altogether? Refine your skills and watch carefully for signs of exhaustion or avoidance - it's always okay to take a break.

At the end of the day, remember why you are doing this: to have fun. The ability to relax and to enjoy your dog - that is the ultimate goal! Now stop reading this book and go play. We'll be here when you get back.

Chapter Sixteen
Problem Solving Your Personal Play

Personal play is a lot of fun, but there can be a steep learning curve. Some dogs are quite resistant to personal play. They might look bored or even uncomfortable. Other dogs are really into personal play – so much so that it becomes painful for the trainer! If you've followed our advice in the previous chapters and are still struggling, read on. This chapter will address the common personal play challenges trainers run across.

Dog Has No Interest

The most common reason that dogs are not interested in personal play is that they feel overwhelmed. This is an excellent time to video your interaction. Pay close attention to your dog's behavior.

Deb is doing a great job of making herself non-threatening, but now Zuri is not interested in play.

Is he showing any avoidance behaviors? Does he turn away from you? Does he avoid eye contact? Is he licking his lips? Does he try to leave the area entirely? Any of these signals indicate that your play technique is frightening your dog rather than appealing to him. The solution is to dial it down a notch! You need to reduce the intensity, so make your movements smaller and quieter. You should also move away from the dog rather than towards him.

If, on the other hand, your dog is watching you calmly but seems disinterested, that is a somewhat different issue. Watch for the tiniest indicators of engagement: ear flicks, slight changes in posture, or the angle at which he tilts his head. Even the smallest tail wag is important to note. When you see any indication that your dog is interested, smile, praise, and approach your dog for a quick pat or a moment of warmth.

When you come home from an absence, pay attention to how you and your dog interact during greetings. If your dog is happy to see you, how do you respond? Pay attention to the pitch of your voice, the words you use, and the way you use your body to move into the house. Also note if your dog is at your front or the side, and how he prefers to greet you. This is a great opportunity to find the behaviors that are most natural to both of you.

In addition to carefully observing your interaction with your dog, you should watch him when he plays with other dogs. See if you can determine his favorite play style. Does he like chase games? If so, run with your dog. Does he love jaw wrestling? Then get your claw hand out. Is he grabbing the other dog's legs or feet? Then go ahead and give that a try!

Greeting at the door.

Still struggling? Try this: Find a private place and turn on some high energy music that you like. Now, start singing and dancing while your dog is in the room (maybe with the assistance of an adult beverage). When you are relaxed and obviously having a good time, you have a great chance of piquing your dog's interest. He may well decide he wants to join you! Any time your dog shows any avoidance, go back to dancing by yourself - the lack of pressure is all many dogs need to choose to stay in the game with you.

Keep in mind that it can take months for a dog to begin to engage in personal play comfortably. Stick with it! Assign a few minutes each day to observing and interacting with your dog; watch carefully and see what it takes to get a reaction. Just remember to match your dog's energy, avoid overwhelming him, and don't become discouraged.

Dog Plays Too Rough or Bites

For some teams, lack of engagement is the least of their problems. Instead, they have dogs who become so excited that play becomes uncomfortable or even painful. It can be difficult to find just the right level of arousal for mutually enjoyable play. This is a tricky balancing act! If the dog is too high, he is likely to engage with his mouth and teeth. If he is too low, he is not interested in engagement at all.

A toy as an intermediary play object can be helpful, especially with puppies. Using a toy will allow your dog to fully express himself without hurting you because it keeps his mouth busy! See how long you can play with the puppy without touching the toy. At first, you'll probably have to tug the toy every few seconds to keep it in the puppy's mouth, but over time you'll notice that you can go almost a full session without touching the toy! When you get to this point, you'll find that your dog has much more self control when you play without a toy present.

With a trained adult dog, redirecting high arousal into work can be very successful. You can encourage play, then send your dog to perform a series of jumps, run through the weaves, or perform another distance behavior, instead of coming into your space. This will help him release some of that built up energy so that he can stay at an optimal level of arousal.

Accidents can happen in play but some dogs are too rough all the time!

To prevent over arousal after a game of chase, ask your dog to fall into work!

Dog Won't Remain Engaged

A problem in the middle of the spectrum between no engagement and too much is when a dog will start playing but then disengages. The truth is, there may not be a problem at all. Because personal play can be physically taxing on both the dog and the trainer, it is very difficult to play well for a long period of time. Excellent play only needs to last for ten or twenty seconds at a time to be effective.

Rather than working on extended periods of play, think in terms of extended periods of engagement. To accomplish this, start up a game of play. Before your dog would normally lose interest, redirect to work or a toy. For the next round, use play to reward the work, but remember to keep it to a short interval.

If your dog actually walks away in the middle of a short play session, it is likely that you have overwhelmed your dog. Try again at a lower level of intensity. Also, consider some different play techniques. For example, if you have been wrestling with a dog who does not like to be touched, then try games that allow the dog to come into your space instead. Let the dog leap around you and chase your hands. See if this experiment keeps your dog engaged.

Another possibility is that some dogs have a very difficult time playing in a space where they normally train and work. They are so distracted by the promise of food or toys that they simply cannot see what you are doing. If this sounds like your dog, play in an area where you have never worked for food or toys before. Start small. Sit on the floor in order to work on basic engagement and praise before you slowly work up to more intensity. If you see progress, move into a larger space, but continue to avoid your regular working space until your dog understands and is interested in personal play.

Handler Doesn't Know How to Combine Personal Play with Toys or Food

This may seem like an odd problem to have since we have emphasized the need to play without any intermediary objects, but there are good reasons you might want to combine personal play with toys or food. Sometimes the dog finds your sudden increase in attentiveness and interaction a bit overwhelming or confusing, especially if your dog is already an adult.

Combining personal play with tugs, balls, or food, particularly during the learning phase, can help a dog become more comfortable with personal play. If your dog has already learned that earning classic rewards means you are pleased, then combining toys or food with play can pave the way to accepting personal play as a reward. Of course, the potential downside is that your dog will learn to go through the motions of play to try to earn the classic reward instead of playing for the joy of engagement.

To combine toys or food with personal play, wait until your dog finds the front of your body or comes into your personal space, and then whip out your toy or food and

*It is totally okay to practice your personal play
with a toy in your dog's mouth.
Just interact with the dog instead of the toy!*

encourage him to chase you to get this classic reward. Do not end by just handing over the cookie; the more energy your dog has to show to get the classic reward, the more value it has.

If your dog gets too aroused during personal play, then you can use the toys or food to redirect a dog's energy from you (often displayed as biting or grabbing) to the external reward. If you use the classic reward in this manner, deliver it quietly and possibly away from you. You want a short break that will help lower his arousal and direct his attention elsewhere. Wait a few seconds to start playing again. It's important that your dog learns to move from excited to calm in a relatively short period of time, and food can be an easy way to teach the skill of arousal control.

Handler Doesn't Know How to Combine Work and Play

Most trainers think that combining work and play is done solely to reward work behaviors, but it can also be extremely useful in developing your personal play technique.

For dogs who like to work and need the structure it provides, play can be challenging because they don't know what is expected of them. This is particularly true for dogs who are not normally very playful, but some dogs can get very nervous when we try to play if they have only experienced structure. For these dogs, we can teach personal play in a more structured way. Show your dog a play-based behavior like lowering your body and stalking and as soon as you have his attention, call him into work. Now switch to a classic reward for a short period, and then offer another play-based behavior. Your dog will begin to recognize that your play moves signal the start of energy and activity, and when he does, you can then engage in play more directly.

Another reason you might want to combine work and play is to provide structure for dogs who generate too much energy in play. By going from play immediately into work, you give them an acceptable place to focus that energy. For example, you might do ten seconds of heeling before slowing down your pace and dropping your body (signaling the beginning of play), snapping off to the right with great glee, and then as the dog approaches, immediately go back into formal heeling again. The more aroused your dog is, the shorter the play breaks will be. If your dog is capable of playing most of the time and only occasionally gets too aroused or rough, you can play for longer stretches before going back into work.

Conclusion

Personal play with your dog is incredibly valuable both as a way to enhance your relationship and as a training tool. If you master techniques that work for both of you, you'll have a motivator and reward that you can use anytime and anywhere - even if you had no intention of training at that time! You will also build energy, engagement, focus and intensity, all while having fun with your canine friend.

Very few trainers take the time to develop personal play as a motivator. It is definitely easier to bring out cookies or toys to encourage desirable behaviors, but we lose so much in terms of personal interaction and relationship building when we constantly add these intermediaries to our interactions. Try using just your expression, voice, posture, and movement instead; you might be surprised at how readily your dog responds. It may be the most fun you have with your dog!

Chapter Seventeen
Introduction to Food Play

Food is a primary motivator for all organisms. As such, it is the most innately powerful choice of reward for many - but not all - dogs. Food drive is closely linked to survival, especially for newborn and very young puppies who must aggressively seek out the only source of food he can eat (mom's milk). A puppy with very low food drive is not likely to live. As a result, even after thousands of years of domestication, most dogs have at least a minimal level of food drive that we can harness for performance work.

As we write this, food is the most popular motivator for many performance trainers. Used well, food will help a dog focus on his task and allow for a rapid accumulation of behaviors. In addition, appropriate use of food will encourage the dog to show energy and joy in his work.

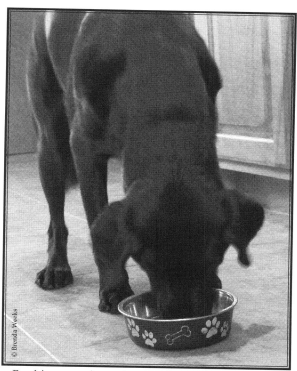

Food is a very important motivator for all animals!

But food play is distinctly different from using food in training. Both have their place in a well-rounded training plan, and in this chapter, we will explain what food play is, how it differs from simply using food in training, and why we think you should take the time to master this skill.

What Is Food Play?

Food play combines the act of eating with elements of play like movement, energy, focus, and fun. Combining these two things brings together the best traits of play with the very strong motivating value of food.

Staci is training Banner with food, but only in one photo is she using food play.
Both photos show great training choices but for different reasons!

Using food in training does NOT mean you are engaging in food play. A trainer who approaches her dog and places a piece of food in his mouth is not playing with her dog, although she is using food in training. The dog is eating without putting out effort to get the food. There is no motion, interaction, or fun involved, even though the dog will still enjoy the food. There is nothing wrong with this; indeed, it might be exactly the right approach for training that dog to do a particular task - but it is NOT food play.

Food play requires energy. It requires movement and enthusiasm. A dog who runs across the yard at full speed in order to chase down a trainer with a cookie is showing many qualities that we associate with play. The dog is engaged with the trainer and moving with speed, energy, and focus. In other words, the trainer has become more than a simple cookie dispenser.

Why Use Food Play?

There are a number of great reasons to use food play.

First, food play builds interest in food as a reinforcer by combining it with play. This is incredibly important for trainers who have dogs with high prey drive but lower food drive. For example, tossing a piece of food away from the dog requires him to chase it in order to eat it. The chase is a clear aspect of predatory behavior that is intrinsically motivating for most dogs. Another example is putting a piece of food under a sofa cushion. If the dog must sniff it out in order to eat it, we can see that eating becomes linked with hunting, another predatory behavior that many dogs enjoy.

Food play also makes each piece of food much more valuable due to the energy and interaction required to get it. Rather than food being an event that takes just seconds to complete (into the mouth and down the hatch), with food play, each piece can take twenty or thirty seconds from the start of the game until it is totally consumed. This entire period is part of the reinforcement and adds great value to the food reward itself.

Chasing a cookie builds food drive!

Another benefit of food play is the way it clearly links the trainer to the food. This happens because most food play requires close trainer involvement through running, throwing, hiding, and so on. Without this, you may have no more value to your dog than a Pez dispenser. While Pez dispenser style feeding clearly has valuable uses in training, it's important to recognize that one Pez dispenser can be easily exchanged for another.

This is not the case in food play. While a dog may take a treat from a stranger, most dogs will not play with a new person - even for food. Play requires a level of trust. Dogs do not chase strangers with food as easily because the dog must know that the game is safe, and that the person wants to engage at such a personal level. As a result, you must work to teach your dog that this level of engagement is both acceptable and desirable.

Finally, food play is fun! Handing over a cookie is certainly satisfying on a basic level for a dog, but engaging in play behaviors is much more enjoyable. Using one's body – running, chasing, leaping - is fun for both dogs and people.

So Food Play is the Best Way to Use Food in Training, Right?

Wrong! Food play is awesome, but there is definitely a place in training for dispensing food Pez dispenser style. When engaged in classic shaping activities (clicker training), you will probably rapidly dispense food in a relatively quiet manner. If you are working on a behavior where you want to get in a very high number of repetitions in a short period of time, simple food delivery will be much more effective than constantly breaking off the session for active food play.

Food play does not make sense when teaching Ridge to stay in position.

Food play does not lend itself to quiet, thoughtful activities, such as when a dog is learning a highly complex behavior that requires concentration. In this instance, food is best used to quietly mark the correct choices in order to keep the dog calm and thoughtful. Quiet food delivery also makes sense when you are practicing stays or other stationary behaviors where you want the dog to stay still as opposed to moving around.

When you are using food to reward for position - where the food is delivered as close as possible to the place where the dog completed the behavior - food play is impractical. For example, if you are teaching a dog to touch a target, the food should be delivered close to the target. In this case, delivering the food between the dog's nose and the target is an effective technique, but it is not food play.

Feeding for emotional comfort is another situation in which food should be used in a controlled and quiet manner. When feeding for emotional comfort (as opposed to learning or practicing behaviors) the purpose of the food is to calm the dog's nervous system. If you use food in a playful fashion, you are actually revving up the dog's nervous system and undoing the calming value of the food.

Finally, it is also important to consider the trainer's mechanical skill level in handling food. If a novice trainer is struggling to simply practice effective food delivery, then she is not yet ready to provide the rewards in a more active manner, even if the dog might benefit from food play.

So When Should I Use Food Play?

Food play is an excellent choice when:

You want to build a love of work in your puppy or young dog.

Most puppies have strong food drives and are naturally playful, making them especially likely to engage in food play without much encouragement from you. This is great because the interaction inherent in food play serves to build up the relationship with the trainer. As a result, the dog learns that it is more than food; it is also about the game. Later on, when we call this game work, your puppy will already think it's great fun!

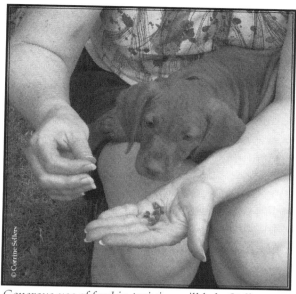

Generous use of food in training will help Stella grow into an enthusiastic adult competitor.

You want to bring energy to your work.

Sully is building energy in his work by chasing food back and forth for his reward.

It is very difficult for a dog to chase you for food and not put out energy, and this energy can then be channeled back into work. The more you play games with food, the more you will build value in the food itself. When a dog has to work hard for a bit of cookie, that cookie develops value both for itself (yum!) and for the process that led to it (effort and energy!). In this way, you build effort, energy, and food desire simultaneously.

Your dog does not value toy play.

Food play is also an excellent choice for dogs who do not value (or have not yet learned to value) toy play. The games that your dog comes to enjoy with food can later be transitioned into the same games with toys. Encourage your dog to love toys, but until he does, use food play when your training would benefit from a game. Remember, you should never try to teach behaviors using a motivator that your dog does not actually want.

Mary Ann can throw food to reward Deacon at a distance.
This is a wonderful use of a cookie in play!

You want to reward your dog at a distance.

Food play is an excellent choice when you want to reward your dog at a distance. For example, if your dog has done a wonderful series of jumps and you want to reward the dog at the end of that sequence, throwing the food to the correct spot will be much faster (and more interesting) than if you were to walk over there to deliver the food.

You want to develop your relationship with your dog.

Food play guarantees that you will be actively involved with your dog, which helps develop your working relationship with your dog. It's also fun, and the more fun you have with your dog in training, the more both of you will look forward to your working sessions. Teams that enjoy their training together are much more likely to find success in dog sports.

You want self-control in addition to drive.

Control and drive-building games are two sides of the same coin. The difference is in who is doing the controlling. If you physically control your dog by holding him back, then you are building drive (and eroding self-control). If you ask the dog to hold himself back through self-control, then you are building impulse control; the release to the reward maintains the dog's interest in the activity. When self-control is added within the context of a game, dogs quickly recognize that they need their trainers. Listening and responding to cues leads to what they want – the cookie!

Asking Lexi to wait for her cookie builds control...and drive!

Selecting Treats for Food Play

The treats you choose for food play will make a big difference in how successful your games are. There are several things you should consider. First, think about the color of the food item. If it blends in with your working space, it will be much harder for the dog to chase and find. Contrasting colors often work best. The size is also important. If it is too big, the dog must chew a lot to eat, which slows down your game. If it's too small, it's hard for the dog to find. Related to size is the weight of the food. Lightweight foods are very hard to throw with any accuracy. Finally, consider how sticky the food is. Sticky treats often stay on your fingers or take time to lick off the floor, causing you to lose the rhythm of the game.

Here are some ideas:

- **Cheese** - easy to throw, shows up well on most surfaces, but can get a bit sticky.

- **Hot dogs** - larger pieces throw well, shows up on most surfaces, easy for dog to pick up.

- **Cheerios** - perfect on dark surfaces, but lightweight and hard to throw. Low calorie.

- **Dog food** - great for overweight dogs or dogs with lower drive for treats but high drive for their dinner.

- **Chicken** - easy to see on dark surfaces, highly palatable. Tends to shred, leaving behind lots of tiny bits that can interrupt the game.

- **Cheetos** - show up very well on a variety of surfaces, but high in calories.

- **Vegetables** soaked in meat juice - Denise's small dog Brito loves tiny slices of carrot soaked in tripe juice; not great for Denise but an excellent choice for a nine pound dog who can't eat too much!

- **Popcorn** - shows up well, low calorie, but lightweight and hard to throw.

Experiment with a variety of foods to see what works best for you, your dog, and the game you want to play. No matter which food you choose, the most important factor is that your dog is motivated to work for it. Without that, you have no way to encourage your dog to engage in the game with you.

Visual Tracking and Maturity

Before we get into the games themselves, we need to take a moment to discuss how maturity affects a dog's ability to play food games. Many of the games that we recommend will require your dog to visually track a fast-moving piece of food, and that ability develops with age. It is perfectly normal for a young puppy to struggle to accurately follow a piece of food skittering across the floor. It's even harder for that same pup to coordinate his eyes and mouth for a game of catch.

You can still play food games with a pup, but you want to make them easier until his nervous system and developmental skills mature and you can play the game at a very advanced level. Remember, games are all about fun, not accuracy. It's okay if your dog doesn't actually catch the food when you throw it!

Conclusion

As we move forward into discussing some specific food games you can play with your dog, remember that there are really only two rules: 1) that your dog actually likes the food you're offering, and 2) that you are both having fun! Both of these things are very important if food play is to be an effective technique for your team.

Puppies often have poor visual tracking so don't throw the cookies too far!

Chapter Eighteen
Food Games

The good news about food play is that most dog and handler teams take to it very quickly. Unlike tug and fetch, food play is a fairly simple mechanical skill, making it easy to learn. In addition, there are a lot of fun ways to play with food - you're really only limited by your imagination!

In this chapter, we are presenting a number of food games, organized by type: moving games, fighting games, and hunting games. All of these games tap into different parts of the prey sequence. Since each dog is unique in his preferred form of play, you'll want to experiment with the games we suggest to discover which ones you and your dog find the most fun.

Dogs who chase toys also tend to enjoy chasing cookies!

MOVING GAMES

Dogs who enjoy games of chase (whether a toy, a squirrel, a cookie, or you) will enjoy these movement-oriented games!

Two Treats Game

Throw a cookie underhanded (as if you're bowling) off to one side. After your dog chases and eats the treat, call your dog excitedly. As he reorients to you, throw another piece of food in the opposite direction.

This game really gets your dog moving! Even shy and inhibited dogs seem to loosen up and really start to run while playing this game. If you always throw the food straight and low, your dog will learn to track your arm motion, which is very useful for go outs, marking gloves, and agility work that requires the dog to watch your hand/arm signals to cue a direction of travel. This game is also an excellent choice if you are in a new environment and you want your dog to relax and play a little before starting formal work. Most dogs find it enjoyable and engaging. It's also an excellent way to reward or release a dog from formal work, or simply to have fun together.

Come and Go Game

Brito loves chasing treats back and forth in the Two Treat Game!

This is similar to the two treat game, but with a recall back to you before you toss the second cookie. Show your dog a treat and toss it forward away from you, verbally encouraging your dog to go get it. Use the same cue word each time. As soon as your dog picks up the cookie, call him back to you. Reward his recall with another tossed treat. Repeat, repeat, repeat.

This game teaches your dog to move away from you with confidence. It also teaches him a cue for taking food on the floor. In addition, it reinforces his recall back to you. This is a fast-paced, exciting game that most dogs really enjoy.

Prey Hand Game

Instead of handing your dog a piece of food, in this game, you'll wiggle your hand like a vibrating mouse! This excites most dogs, making them much more intense and focused about taking food from you.

Start by standing facing your dog. Your fingers should be facing forward, at your dog's nose height, and about one or two inches away. Quickly start to vibrate your hand while keeping your arm close your body; only your hand, from the wrist to fingers, should be moving. Now move away from your dog, but instead of moving your arm backwards, walk your feet backwards or in a circle away from your dog, allowing your dog to chase your fingers. Watch for the moment that your dog surges forward. That is the point at which your dog wins the food.

This game is particularly useful for dogs who are tentative about taking food. In

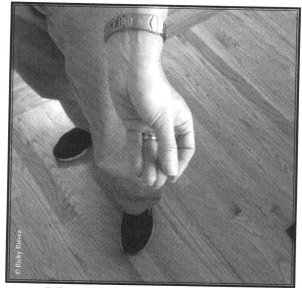 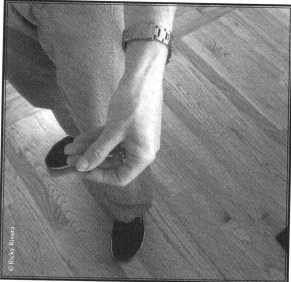

When using your hand like prey, your fingers are facing up and your wrist moves back and forth.

addition to encouraging the dog to relax and chase the food, it helps him be comfortable while close against your body. However, this game may not be a good choice for dogs who are very rough or grabby when they take food from their trainer.

It's Raining Cheese! Game

Place a cookie in your mouth and drop the food from your mouth to your dog. We recommend cheese because it has good visual contrast and does not taste disgusting. At first, the food will probably fall to the floor, but after a few times, most dogs start trying to catch it before it falls. In a matter of days or weeks, your dog should be able to catch the food before it hits the ground. This skill will be useful for rewarding precision sits in front of your body. Some dogs are slow to learn to catch, so be patient.

Trainer as Prey Game

In this game, both the trainer AND the food are moving. Instead of throwing the food, run straight away and let your dog chase you. When your dog catches you, encourage him to come into your hands for a cookie. A variation on this is to have your dog

Even small dogs can catch food!

jump up to your hands for his cookie.

If you gently push the dog away as you run off with the cookie, you'll also encourage your dog's opposition reflex – valuable for many exercises in later training. Another option, if you have a helper, is to have that person hold your dog back by the collar or around the front of the chest while you run away. When your dog shows eagerness, your helper should release the dog to chase you down. The reward is a game of chase and a cookie!

Brito loves being held back so that he can chase Denise when she explodes forward!

To make this game even more effective and rewarding, you can combine it with any of the games described above. For example, after your dog catches you, encourage your dog to either chase the cookie in your hand, jump up to your hand to get it, or toss it forward to maintain the momentum. This will encourage your dog to continue making an effort to get the cookie even after he catches you!

Jump for Food

Why hand a cookie to a dog when you can have him jump up for it? Dogs enjoy using their bodies. If you doubt that, simply watch the sport of agility to see how much fun it is for the dogs to move, run, and jump!

The first time you ask for a jump, only ask for a few inches. You can increase the height he jumps over time, until your dog must make effort to reach the food. Greater effort leads to greater energy!

When you ask your dog to jump, the food target should be predictable. Don't move your hand as the dog jumps or he will start snatching the food from your hands, which will hurt your fingers. You will also want to practice with both hands and from different angles. For example, ask your dog to jump up while facing you, and the next time start the dog from your side. In addition to having fun and adding movement to your training, you are also working on your dog's targeting skills.

Raika loves to jump up for her treats!

Cookie Race

This game is really fun for all involved. To play, toss a cookie straight ahead while restraining your dog by his chest, collar, or hips. After a verbal build up ("ready... set....go!"), release your dog and race him to the cookie! Always let the dog win this game at first to help build his confidence. In fact, the very second the dog passes you, stop running forward and immediately reverse, which will encourage the dog to come back as quickly as possible to play the game again. If you continue to run after your

Raika loves the Cookie Race Game, especially when she wins!

dog when he has passed you, he may perceive you as chasing him down, which is very threatening for many dogs.

If you have a confident and motivated dog, you can add some control to this game by asking for a stay first. If you have a really fast dog, this also lets you have a head start towards the cookie before you release him - but even with a confident dog, he should win 99% of the time!

Another variation of the cookie race game is to ask your dog for a specific position before you release him. Instead of saying "ready... set... go!" start with something the dog is normally fluent at performing (like a down or a sit). At first your dog will be surprised by your request, so start easy. You can lower the arousal level of this game by placing the food on the ground instead of tossing it. As soon as your dog responds and moves into the cued position, send him to the food.

Zen Bowl Games

Cookie race games can also become zen bowl games. The zen bowl starts as a self control game. Place a piece of food in the bowl and show it to your dog. Slowly lower the bowl towards the ground. If your dog holds still, quickly put the bowl down and give your dog verbal permission to get the cookie. If your dog tries to get to the bowl before your verbal cue, move it up and away from him. There are no verbal cues to wait or stay for this exercise. If your dog holds still, the bowl moves to the ground. If he moves towards the bowl, it moves up and away from him. Over a few sessions, most dogs figure out that they can make you put the bowl on the ground by holding still and waiting for a verbal release.

When using a Zen Bowl, make sure the dog sees you drop the cookie in!

Once your dog has a basic understanding of the zen bowl, you can then use it as a target for your dog to run towards, just like the race to the cookie game. Set out the bowl with some food inside, move away from it with your dog, and encourage him to race you towards it. You can add distance to this game very quickly. Through a number of repetitions, you can hold back more and more until you are simply sending your dog to the bowl. This is a nice approximation of a send away or go-out behavior.

You can also use the zen bowl as a distraction during training. Set it out but ask your dog to do something else first (start with something very easy), then send him to the bowl as his reinforcer. Eventually you can ask for more and more difficult behaviors and for more duration in behaviors before you release him to the bowl.

Fight Games

The following games are all designed to build "fight." The goal is to give the dog permission to push you around a little, just enough so that the dog is willing to engage you as an equal partner! We want active working dogs, and building fight might be just the ticket for your wallflower. Please note, though, that these games may not be appropriate for dogs who are struggling with impulse control, or for handlers who are not comfortable encouraging more assertive behavior in their larger or stronger dogs.

The Hand Push Game is good for very fragile dogs who are just starting out with food games.

Denise gently blocks Brito from the cookie which builds his drive and determination to get it!

Hand Push

This activity is designed to help soft or tentative dogs build up their confidence, develop pushiness, and become comfortable in your space.

Hold a treat in your fist, hold it out towards your dog, and wiggle it a little while verbally encouraging him to get it. At first, open your hand if your dog nudges it even the smallest amount, but over time, ask your dog to push your hand for several seconds and with as much body engagement as possible before you give him the treat.

The Blocking Game

This is a great game for more tentative dogs who need to develop sureness, confidence, and power, but it's not appropriate for dogs who already show plenty of drive and self confidence.

Begin by holding the cookie in one hand on an open palm. Then, with your other hand (or arm or finger, depending on the size of the dog), gently block your dog from getting to the food. This is not a self control exercise, so verbally encourage your dog to get that cookie! If your dog shows any attempt to overcome your resistance – even the smallest push against your littlest finger - immediately remove the block and let your dog get the cookie.

As your dog's skills progress, encourage active problem solving! Instead of blocking with your hand, use your entire arm, and encourage your dog to find a way over, under, or through your block! Praise and encourage effort at every step of the game! Remember, you should be verbally cheering your dog on the entire time - it's you and the dog against your arm!

The Slingshot Game

This game uses the opposition reflex to encourage your dog to actively resist you and explode forward upon your release, much like a slingshot. It also helps teach an active release to work. It can be used at the start line towards the first obstacle in agility, the dumbbell retrieve in obedience, or a speedy and enthusiastic go-out behavior.

To play, throw a cookie a couple feet in front of you and hold your dog back by the chest, ruff, or collar. Do NOT give a stay cue; you want your dog to actively resist you and explode forward upon your release. Immediately before releasing your dog, slightly increase the pressure against his chest. Think of a slingshot; pulling back should cause your dog to brace his body and then shoot forward when he's

The opposition reflex used in the Slingshot Game can be very powerful for building forward drive!

released. Remember to push your dog away from the direction you want him to travel. In this case, you want your dog to surge towards a cookie being thrown straight ahead, so the dog should be pulled directly backwards from the food before the release.

It's important that your dog understands you aren't really taking him away from the food and that you really do want him to fight back! If your dog seems to be struggling with this, as you pull back, encourage him verbally by saying "ready?!" and then "get it get it get it!" when you release him. You want your dog to believe that his resistance caused you to let go; he was too strong for you!

Start small! The amount of tension should initially be so minor that an observer could not tell that you're applying tension. Once your dog understands the game, you can use more resistance to teach your dog to focus very hard and resist the pressure with his entire body. Over time, you will find that you have to hold your dog quite firmly to prevent an early release. If your dog shows a loss of drive or discomfort at any time, change how you're restraining him as he's telling you that he doesn't like what you're doing.

Food Stuffed Toys

Games of tug are essentially fight games, but not all dogs enjoy playing tug. Of course, we hope that you've helped your dog develop a love of tug by following our advice earlier in this book, but if you've given up on building the game of tug organically and have instead decided to pair toys with food, you may enjoy using a food-stuffed toy.

Most dogs really enjoy working for an interactive toy that holds food on the inside.

These toys are designed to be filled with food and then used as an interactive toy. They are distinct from food dispensing toys like a Buster Cube or the Kong Wobbler, which do not require the handler's assistance in order to play with them. Instead, they look more like a tug toy except with a pocket that food can be stuffed in.

We do not recommend these toys if you are actively attempting to teach your dog the game of tug with a prey object because the smell of the food often prevents dogs from playing for the sake of the activity itself. The dog ends up focusing too much on the food and not enough on play!

These toys are also a unique and enjoyable twist on the traditional tug game for dogs who do enjoy tug.

Hunt Games

Hunt games allow dogs to use their noses - and we know that dogs love to use their noses! Hunt games are appropriate for all types and temperaments of dogs. Hunt games allow dogs to develop a feeling of control over the environment. When a dog feels a sense of mastery and control, he will naturally come to value and enjoy the activities more. This feeling of control over the environment will increase a dog's confidence level and his enthusiasm for the games that you play together, including training.

Brito is learning to play the body search game on leash. The food could be anywhere on Denise!

Body Search

Start by sitting on the floor with your dog facing you. Hold your dog back - do not use a stay command - and place a cookie right between your knees while your dog is watching. Let him go with a "find it!" cue, and let him grab the cookie. As he shows confidence and understanding, start pulling your knees together so he has to use his nose and dig a bit to get to the cookie. This adds an element of fight to the basic hunt game.

When he knows how to search in the space between your knees, start adding other spaces, like under your ankles or in your pockets. If you play this game while sitting in a chair, you can add any hiding spaces that are on the chair as well as on your body.

We suggest playing this game with your dog on a leash so that you can use it at dog shows. This game is extremely valuable before entering the competition ring since it takes up almost no space and helps mildly nervous dogs relax. Eventually, you can change this game to having your dog find whatever ring objects you will be using in competition. For example, if you are going to compete in AKC obedience, hide a glove or a dumbbell on your body and let your dog find it. This game never fails to put Denise's dogs in a good mood before entering the ring.

Cookie Hide and Seek

This is one of the best options for building food drive in dogs who have a strong hunt drive. Instead of handing over a cookie, show the cookie to your dog and walk off slowly and with a slight crouch to your posture – this stalking picture should get your dog's attention! Leave your dog confined in an area or ask a helper to hold your dog back and hide the cookie somewhere in the room. In the early stages, you'll want your dog to see you do this. Return to your dog and release him with plenty of excitement in your voice, encouraging your dog to "find it!"

When your dog is showing enthusiasm and understanding of the game, make the hiding places harder to find. Eventually your dog will become an expert at this game and you will run out of places to hide your cookies!

If your dog enjoys this game, adding it to regular training rewards can be extremely exciting and motivating. For example, if you are doing a session of scent articles, you might reward a correct choice by throwing the cookie behind random objects in your training area. Searching for the food makes that cookie a lot more valuable than just handing it over. It also releases the stress of a formal session, which keeps the training session enjoyable for both of you.

Brito found his cookie!

Conclusion

As positive reinforcement trainers, we have moved far beyond the point of just tossing cookies at a dog for desired behaviors and are now learning how to use both food and play in highly sophisticated and ingenious ways. Used properly, food play can help develop confidence and enthusiasm in dogs who need it. It can also be used to either increase drive and motivation or encourage self-control and thoughtfulness - or both.

Pay attention to what your dog needs to focus on for any particular situation or behavior. Choose the food game that encourages the mental and emotional state your dog needs. When in doubt, always go for enthusiasm and excitement.

Because food games combine the best aspects of both food and play, they are truly the best of both worlds.

Chapter Nineteen
Problem Solving Food Play

When it comes to food play, there are really only two problems you might encounter: a dog who has very little interest in food, and a dog who has too much interest in food. Far and away, the former problem is more common, so we will spend most of our time troubleshooting the problem of a dog with low food drive. Very high food drive may create some impulse control issues, but we don't consider that a food play problem.

Give some thought to your choice of food for your dog!

Low Food Drive

While food is a primary reinforcer for most creatures, some dogs truly eat to live, rather than live to eat. While this is the exception to the rule, it comes up often enough that the issue of low food drive needs to be addressed. Here are some reasons that a dog may not seem interested in food.

Dog is Overfed

Your dog might not be low in food drive at all. He might simply be overfed and therefore not particularly interested in eating anything else. Make sure your dog is at a healthy weight for a performance dog. If you cannot feel your dog's ribs and hip bones, a diet might be in order. If you're not sure, check with your vet. Be sure to explain that you are interested in performance events for your dog. Vets are often loathe to tell people that their dogs are overweight, but if you explain your interests, they are likely to be more honest with you. If the vet says your dog could lose a few pounds, take it seriously.

Some dogs do not lack food drive; they are simply overweight.

Food Isn't Valuable Enough

Be sure you are using food that has value to your dog. If kibble is your dog's daily fare, it may not be good enough for your games. It's time to up the ante. Experiment with different foods until you find those that work for your dog. In addition to trying out regular dog treats, don't forget to check out your refrigerator. Small bites of hot dog, cheese, and last night's dinner are extremely appealing to most dogs. Since dogs working for food tend to be thinking in terms of dessert rather than dinner, make sure you're offering a worthwhile taste!

Maisy indicates with her gaze which food she finds more appealing

Dog Gets Food for Free

Instead of giving meals to your dog from a food bowl, consider having your dog work for his meals. In addition to the behaviors you want to work on, play food games like tossing kibble, jumping for kibble, and chasing you for kibble. At the end of the day, your dog should be given any leftover food either in great handfuls directly from you or out of his food bowl. You should NEVER allow your dog to go hungry to satisfy your performance interest, but there's no reason you can't ask your dog to put out some energy to get his meal.

Most dogs really enjoy working for their meals!

Environment is too Exciting

Check out the environment. Some dogs aren't really low in food drive - they are just more interested in the alternatives! If your dog finds the smells on the ground and the sights in the distance absolutely fascinating, play your games in lower stimulation environments until you develop your dog's interest in working. Also, it's fairly common for puppies and young working dogs to be more interested in the environment rather than you. This gets better with time if you are patient, so don't push your dog beyond his abilities.

Dog is Worried

Nervous or worried dogs often refuse to eat. Whether or not your dog is comfortable taking food is a good gauge of how comfortable he is in the environment. This is not an issue of food drive; it's an issue of emotional comfort. It is a bad idea to try to train your dog if he is feeling so nervous that he can't play food games. Change your environment to one that your dog is more comfortable in, and slowly increase the challenge level as your dog shows you he can manage. With time and patience you can move into more challenging environments.

Dog Won't Visually Track or Catch Food

If your dog won't watch or catch food, it may not be an issue of low food drive. Instead, it is likely that he simply hasn't developed the maturity and coordination needed. This is extremely common in puppies and it almost always improves with age. Allow your dog's vision, tracking skills, and reflexes to develop. Soon he will be tracking and catching food, even as you spit it from your mouth!

Some dogs are simply poorer than others at visually tracking food, even as adults. First, check and make sure there is no hair obstructing your dog's vision. If this is a possibility, tie his hair up during working sessions. Use food that rolls and falls more slowly. Popcorn and cheese puffs are very good choices for slower moving options. Food that contrasts in color with the floor will also be helpful, and you'll want to be sure that there is absolutely nothing else on the floor to provide distractions. Any small pieces of paper, leaves, or other scraps will make it harder for your dog to find the food.

Make sure your dog can see the food!

If you think your dog is capable of catching the food but lacks the motivation to grab it, stop allowing your dog to pick it up off the floor. Either it is caught in the air or you pick it up yourself. If that is not motivation enough to get him catching food, then it's likely that your dog really is doing his best and he's just not terribly coordinated yet. Keep trying and the time is likely to come when he will be catching all that you throw.

Dog is More Interested in Playing than Eating

Food play is perfect for a dog who prefers playing to eating! Just because your dog isn't interested in a piece of food from your hand does not mean he won't be interested in catching that same food as it goes skittering across the floor. Combine food with games of hunt, prey, and fight to see if that increases his overall interest in working for food.

When Deb's Papillon, Copper, was older and less interested in food in general, he would still eat if she played the two treats game with him. She was able to get many meals into him by adding the excitement of a chase game to his food.

Too Much Food Drive

If your dog has never met a morsel he didn't like, you have a different problem. Your dog might be mauling you by grabbing food out of your hands, nipping at your pockets, and knocking you over to get anything he can. He might be so rough that he's biting you - and bites hurt, even when they're an accident!

If you do you not feel like you are in control of the games when you get out food, it's time to create a plan of action. Trainers who are nervous about being hurt or who start holding the food high in the air end up much worse off than trainers who are in control. Put aside the drive building and focus on the control options. Instead of having your dog push into your hand to get the food, wait until the dog backs away from your hand. Instead of holding your dog back by the collar to increase opposition reflex, use a wait cue.

Just be sure that you don't implement so much control that the dog ends up a frustrated mess - or so little that he isn't thinking at all. Follow the Goldilocks

Most dogs love food but they may need some impulse control training to channel their interest.

rule and find the "just right" amount so your dog can think clearly yet still keep his impulses in check.

Conclusion

Keep it up! The tendency to give up if something doesn't work right away is one of the biggest reasons dogs don't play – with toys, food, or people. If you think a skill has value, then be prepared to work on it. Take the time to learn to use food effectively. Use food to teach behaviors in a calm and thoughtful manner, rewarding for position as appropriate. At the same time, make sure you are also using food to have fun with your dog. You'll be teaching skills which you'll value later on, such as the ability to visually track food, to use the nose to find food, and to jump, run, and exert energy for a reward. All of these skills will serve you well as your training progresses.

Chapter Twenty
Wrapping Up & Moving On

So, how many ways can you motivate a dog to interact with you in an enthusiastic and enjoyable way, both inside and outside of formal training? Now that you've read this book, we hope that you agree with us when we say, "Quite a few!"

Motivational interactions with our dogs are often not intuitive to human players. What's more, while play seems like a simple concept, good play depends on the human having good mechanical skills. This is why we have written an entire book on the topic! We have provided pages of detailed discussion and photo illustrations in this book to make the topic as clear as possible. And we've provided you with a new mantra: **What would the squirrel do?**

At the same time, we hope that you've also grasped the importance of the art of playing. Do your play interactions feel right for your team? If not, what does your intuition suggest instead? Have you selected the right motivator at the right time? Are you playing for too long, too little, or just right? Are you getting the maximum value out of your motivators? Because the mechanical skills of play can never be completely separated from the art of play, we'd like to add a second mantra to hold alongside the first: **Are we having fun yet?**

Even with food as the motivator - the staple of many trainers - food play is not as straightforward as it might initially appear. While quietly handing over a cookie has a place in our training arsenal, the interactive use of food also has a place! When starting a training session, you need to take a moment to look at the dog in front of you and make choices that help you succeed within that interaction. Should this cookie be used to build drive and interactive engagement, or is it time to consider self control? Or is it time to master the drive/self control dichotomy, where the explosive release builds both drives and control simultaneously?

The Dog Sports Skills Series is being developed to help trainers understand training for competition dog sports at a very fundamental level. So far, we have written three books on the topic, yet we've offered almost nothing about the specific competition behaviors. This is not an oversight on our part! Indeed, we would argue that the foundation we are laying now is the human foundation - the knowledge base that will allow you

to lay your dog's training foundation with compassion, understanding, and excellence. If you enter your dog's foundation training with an engaged and comfortable working partner (Book 1), a strong understanding of how to use motivators most effectively to develop learning, cooperation, and skills (Book 2), and both the technical and intuitive skills needed to create maximum value with each training or playful interaction with your dog (Book 3), then you will be able to give your dog the gifts of clarity in the training process, reasonable expectations, mutual enjoyment, and compassion.

Perfection in skill training is not required - your dog will work hard to meet you halfway, even when you make technical mistakes. But a clear understanding of what you wish to accomplish, how you might get there, and an eye to your dog's emotional well-being will allow you to reach your goals in almost any sport with your dog as a willing and engaged partner.

We hope that as you consider ways to add playful interactions to your day, you will hold a picture of excellence in your mind. If you know what you would like to achieve and how it might look, then you will begin to see why the human foundation - your understanding of the entire learning process - is more important than any specific skill training for your dog, and is irrevocably linked to all of the topics that we have presented so far in this series.

Notes:

Notes:

© Scott Johnston

Notes:

Notes:

Made in the USA
Columbia, SC
20 September 2017